THE EIGHT *FIRST* WORDS OF CHRIST

Michael A. Salsbury, MFA

To Jenna, Thank you for your friendship and support. May God bless you richly! Matt. 28:18-20

Michael Salsbury, MFA
PAPA MIKE

MIKE SALSBURY MINISTRIES
Creatively Communicating Christ

MIKE SALSBURY MINISTRIES
mikesalsburyministries@gmail.com

The Eight *First* Words of Christ

Copyright © 2024 by Michael A. Salsbury, MFA

All rights reserved. No part of this publication may be reproduced, stored in a retrieval system, or transmitted in any form by any means, electronic, mechanical, photocopy, recording, or otherwise, without the prior permission of the publisher, except as provided for by USA copyright law.

Cover design: James Vollmer
Interior Design: Dario Ciriello
Cover image: Pisit Heng

First edition 2024

Scripture quotations are from the ESV® Bible (The Holy Bible, English Standard Version®), © 2001 by Crossway, a publishing ministry of Good News Publishers. Used by permission. All rights reserved. The ESV text may not be quoted in any publication made available to the public by a Creative Commons license. The ESV may not be translated in whole or in part into any other language.

All emphases in Scripture quotations have been added by the author.

ISBN: 979-8333-4026-46
Published by Mike Salsbury Ministries

Mike Salsbury Ministries is a non-profit organization in partnership with The Cause.

To my neighbors, Paul and Tony, who mowed my lawn so I could write

To Comins Community Church Berean Sunday School Class, who encouraged me to write even as I teach

And to Sandy, Mary, Diane, Laura, Michelle, Lenore, and Dario, My writing group

IYKYK

CONTENTS

INTRODUCTION	5
CHAPTER ONE	9
CHAPTER TWO	23
CHAPTER THREE	33
CHAPTER FOUR	41
CHAPTER FIVE	53
CHAPTER SIX	67
CHAPTER SEVEN	79
CHAPTER EIGHT	87
CHAPTER NINE	107
CHAPTER TEN	119
CHAPTER ELEVEN	129
ACKNOWLEDGMENTS	137
ABOUT THE AUTHOR	140

INTRODUCTION

Can we all just freely admit that many great ideas occur in the shower?

There I was, one or two Sundays after our annual celebration of Jesus' resurrection, when the phrase "the seven last words of Christ" popped into my mind; and the next thought suddenly struck me: "Wait a minute! We always have to qualify that phrase with "from the cross" because those were *not* really Jesus' "last" words. He spoke to His followers again after His resurrection and right up until His ascension. I wonder... what were Jesus' *first* seven words?" Of course, I immediately dismissed speculation of Jesus' *actual* first words —mama, da-da, bubba, sissy, hi, bye-bye, please, thank you, all in Aramaic, of course – as of little interest in the great scheme of things; but what were his first seven words "out of the *tomb*"?

Of course, what have come to be called "The Seven Last Words of Christ" are not actually mere words at all but rather full sayings, generally brief, encompassing just a thought or two as Jesus suffered in agony while hanging on the cross. I believe I was first introduced to the concept of "The Seven Last Words of Christ" during my college vocal music studies, when I first learned of classical composer Joseph Haydn's oratorio based on the seven sayings. I have subsequently studied the seven sayings devotionally throughout my career as both a pastor and theatre artist and have come to think of them as common knowledge among believers of all stripes; however, they are probably more commonly known primarily in Catholic, Lutheran, and more mainline Protestant traditions than they are among charismatics, fundamentalists, and evangelicals (to paint with some very broad brushes). I will, therefore, open this presentation with a review of "The Seven Last Sayings of Christ from the Cross."

If you are going through this study devotionally or your pastor is preaching it as a series between Easter and Pentecost, may I suggest reading Chapter 1 as part of your Good Friday observance?

Once dried and dressed from my shower, I sat down to my devotions for a quick exploration before Sunday School and church: what might we consider to be Jesus's first sayings from His resurrection to His ascension, and how many were there? Without even looking, I knew that Jesus appeared many more than seven times after His resurrection, but I also knew that Scripture does not record what He spoke at each of those appearances. Over the next hour, I was amazed to discover that there were at least seven occasions between Christ's resurrection and ascension when we have recorded what He spoke on those occasions. A devotional is born! Then I noticed we have indeed seven weeks from Easter to Pentecost in which we might consider those words. A potential sermon series is born!

Why a sermon series? In my opinion, one of the ultimate losses of the Protestant Reformation was a movement away from a common Church liturgy. One can easily see the unifying value in a local church studying together the same passages of Scripture devotionally throughout the week, providing a common ground for discussion of God's Word when we gather. On a broader scale, what if all the churches in a community, regardless of denominational affiliation, were studying the same Scripture every Sunday, even if for so short a period as seven weeks? What might the conversations be in the markets and stores and office buildings, and schools and fitness centers? What if all the churches in a given denomination, conference, or fellowship were doing so? How much greater would be the grounds for unity when they gathered together regionally or annually? How much more information will the sheep retain if they have read a meditation on the Scripture ahead of the shepherd's message covering the same, especially if the shepherd then brings his own unique perspective to the words herein? I trust that pastors will feel free to use what the Holy Spirit has taught me to launch their own studies and thoughts on these Words of our Lord and deepen and develop these vital messages for their own congregations.

I should hasten to add that subsequent study revealed *eight* occasions in which Christ spoke; but you know, once a shower idea is confirmed devotionally, it's very difficult to let it go. What I thought were the final two occasions according to the harmony I was using, one in Galilee and one in Jerusalem, were both messages of commissioning so I had planned to combine them in chapter 9. Because the message in Jerusalem includes Jesus' exhortation for His followers to wait in Jerusalem for the outpouring of the Holy Spirit, I thought it appropriate to wrap up the devotional on Pentecost Sunday.

The Word of God, however, is living and active; and God refuses the beautiful boxes in which we so often hope to wrap Him. When I began writing Chapter 9, I discovered first that Luke 24:44-49 actually belonged earlier in the narrative as part of Word Four; and then I discovered that Dr. Luke's record of Jesus words in Acts 1:3-8 is likely the transcript for Jesus' appearance to the eighty-two or eighty-four apostles that Paul wrote of in I Corinthians 15:7. "Let God be true and every man a liar." The bow on this package isn't as neat as I might have hoped, but I hope you'll enjoy the read all the same. Maybe Word Eight will make a great Father's Day message! Or Ascension Day is the Thursday before Pentecost…

Whether you have come to this book independently as a devotional study or have been introduced to it by your pastor as a corporate church devotional, I trust you will approach it prayerfully, asking the Lord to reveal His truths to you personally from these first words of our Lord out of the grave and prior to His ascension.

Are you searching for someone or something you once had and are now missing? Does your current situation have you frightened and anxious? Do you have trouble understanding how different parts of the Bible connect to one another? Are you upset and restless, disconnected from the Holy Spirit? Are you distressed and uneasy, trying to believe what you cannot see or even imagine? Are you having trouble following Jesus? Are you stagnant and staid, busily living your life but not making any impact on the world for the kingdom of God? Do you feel powerless to reach out to your neighbor next door, let alone your neighbors at the far ends of the world? Then hear the first eight words of the Lord!

CHAPTER ONE

The Seven Last Words of Christ: A Review

The blood. The blood was everywhere: in His mouth, in His nose, dripping from His still ringing ears. His left eye was swollen shut, sealed with drying blood; and through His right eye, the world was tinted pink with blood. How much had He already lost as the blood seeped into His own clothes the soldiers had hastily thrown over His sliced and beribboned back? How much could He lose before death took Him. No, He had to make it to His cross.

A heavy beam of hardwood fell across His shoulders, grinding into His lashed and bloody back and driving Him to the ground, scraping dirt and dust into His already bloodied knees. Immediately, rough hands stretched out his arms and lashed ropes around His wrists, pinning His hands to the back and bottom of the beam. The soldiers ripped Him from the ground, set Him unsteadily on His feet, and shoved Him stumbling forward. His pink tinged vision narrowed and began to close as He felt the blood drain from His head. He barely felt His cheek smash into the dirt and the beam crush His spine as He fell unrestrained to the ground.

As if from a great distance, He heard shouting and protests, a scuffle, and then – all thanks to the Father! – that burred beam lifted from His back. He coughed as the air rushed back into His lungs, and his hands found a way to push Himself up. Again, rough hands pulled Him to His feet, and He found Himself peering at a frightened Libyan, by dress and skin, who now carried the cross beam that was His. He put His arm around the strong man's back and helped as best He could to carry at least some of weight as they haltingly took one step and then the next toward His death.

As they walked, a large crowd followed them, including women who mourned and wailed for Him. As they moved further down the road and His head cleared, He turned to the women and said, "Daughters of Jerusalem, don't cry for Me. Weep for yourselves and your children because the sorts of times are coming when you will think barren women are really blessed women. The time is coming when people will wish for avalanches to bury them. If your leaders will do this when the Kingdom is young and green, imagine the retribution when the Kingdom comes of age."

"Keep moving there!" The butt of a spear cracked across His backside, propelling Him forward, He stumbled and plunged forward to catch up to the great Libyan, passing the two other insurrectionists and thieves who were to be executed along with Him. They had come to the foot of a hill, and now all clambered to its summit for the crucifixions.

On the top of the hill, they found three uprights lying on the ground. Soldiers shoved Him toward the middle upright. They roughly stripped His clothes off Him, ripping open His scabs and wounds afresh; and He felt the blood flow freely, unabated, down His backside and the back of His legs. A soldier shoved a cup of wine, gall, and myrrh to His lips; but the smell revolted Him, and He had no desire to be drugged in His agony. He covered his mouth with one hand, lowered the other, and dropped to His knees in an effort to hide His shame, but a soldier's boot shoved Him on His back in the dust, exposing His nakedness to the morning sun. They had relieved the Libyan of His crossbeam and affixed it to the upright, and now He crawled with all His will to lie down on the rude rack of torture. He stretched His arms out on the crossbeam, the soldiers bound his forearms to the wood; He opened His palms as wide as possible so the expert executioners could find the precise point to nail the spikes through His hands; He crossed His feet with His stronger leg below the weaker so He could push off the nail through His feet to expand His lungs for breath. Finally, the soldiers lifted the cross and His body up from the earth and let the whole bloody mess drop with a joint-rending thud into the hole dug for it. Crucified…

A Prayer for Forgiveness
"Father, forgive them because they don't know what they're doing…"

I would argue that this is the most powerful prayer of forgiveness ever spoken; and once we place ourselves at the Cross of Christ, whether Jew or Gentile, it was spoken over us. The first sight to meet His eye after being raised on the cross was the four Roman soldiers who had just nailed

THE EIGHT *FIRST* WORDS OF CHRIST

Him to His cross, now gathering at his feet to gamble over his bloody clothes – His sandals, His sash, His cloak, His belt, and His blood-sodden tunic, which they decided not to tear. Little did the soldiers know that the blood in those clothes was already at work saving and healing the world.

"Father, forgive them because they don't know what they're doing...."

Next to enter His purview were the cries of the insurrectionists on either side of Him, at first both mocking and insulting Him along with the crowd. They were certainly both patriotic Jews who would have come to see, as Simon the Zealot did, that the Messiah would not first come with military force to overthrow the Romans, had they only been exposed to Him and His teaching sooner.

"Father, forgive them because they don't know what they're doing...."

A servant whom Jesus recognized to be from Pilate's house brought a white-washed board to the top of the hill and gave it to the centurion, who read the words on the sign and strode straight to the foot of Jesus' cross. He ordered the soldiers to pause their gambling and hang the sign at the top of Jesus' cross. One set a ladder against the cross and steadied it with a second while a third climbed the ladder to hang the sign for the world to see. Pilate had written it in Latin, Greek, and the contemporary Hebrew dialect of Aramaic: *Jesus of Nazareth: King of the Jews*.

"Father, forgive them because they *really* don't know what they're doing...."

People passing by on the road below the hill shouted insults up at Him: "You who were going to destroy the temple and rebuild it in in three days, save yourself." "If You are really the 'Son of God, come down off the cross and save yourself." The chief priests, elders, and Torah teachers, who had climbed the hill with Him to be certain His execution was carried out properly, also mocked Him: "He 'saved' others, but he can't save himself!" "If He's the King of Israel, the 'Messiah' as he claims, let him come down from the cross; *then* we will see and believe that miracle." "If God wants Him, let God rescue Him, since He claimed to be His Son."

"Father, forgive them because they don't know what they're doing...."

One of the criminals who hung there beside Him continued to defame Jesus. "If you are the Messiah, save yourself and us!"

"Father, forgive him because he doesn't know what he's doing...."

As fallen humans, one of the most difficult things God asks us to do is to forgive people who have wronged us. Even after more than fifty years of following Jesus, I can name a handful of people – family members, employers, pastors, politicians – whom I still have trouble forgiving or perhaps better "*keeping* them on my forgiveness list" because some sins have repercussions that last throughout our lifetimes. When Jesus taught us to pray, however, he told us to ask God for forgiveness in the same way as we forgive others (Matt. 6:12). Since we all need forgiveness, we all need to be forgiving (Matt. 6:14-15). He tells us to forgive others, even for the same sin, not just once or twice but countless times in the course of life (Matt. 18:21-22).

What I find most encouraging in Jesus' first "last" word from the cross is the *reason* for forgiveness: "... because they don't know what they're doing." They were ignorant. Jesus forgave even those who knew they were being rude or cruel or jealous or (like Pilate) killing an innocent man because they didn't really recognize how greatly they were sinning, how infamous their actions, how notorious they would become for all time. When I place that reason on my family or employers or pastors or even politicians – "Father, forgive them because they don't *really* know what they're doing…." (even if I think that maybe, in some ways, they did know what they were doing) – it makes it easier to keep them forgiven. Try Jesus' first "last" Word on for size and see if it doesn't help you to forgive others as well.

A Promise to a Repentant Criminal
"I tell you the truth: today, you will be with Me in Paradise."

I mentioned the two insurrectionists hurling insults at Jesus among those about whom Jesus said, "Father, forgive them because they don't know what they're doing…."; but the longer they hung together on their separate crosses, the more one of those murdering thieves began to have a change of heart. Eventually, he rebuked his brother in rebellion, asking, "Don't you fear God since we're all under the same sentence here? You and I are being justly punished, getting what our actions deserve; but this man has done nothing wrong!

Then he said, "Jesus, remember me when You come into Your kingdom."

Jesus answered him: "I tell you the truth: today, you will be with Me in Paradise."

I can think of no greater commentary on this passage than Allistair Begg's preaching concerning this thief on the cross. In a sermon entitled "The Power and Message of the Cross," preached at Baylor University's first National Preaching Conference in 2019[1], he made the point that the thief had experienced neither catechism nor baptism. He was cussing out Jesus one minute and asking Him to remember him when He became king the next minute. He imagines the angels quizzing the confused man about how he made it into heaven, and the man is completely ignorant. They quiz him about doctrines like justification by faith and the doctrine of Scripture and finally, in utter frustration, ask him on what basis is he in heaven, to which the thief replies:

"The man on the middle cross said I could come."

That is the *only* answer *any* of us can give. When asked why we should be allowed into heaven, if our answer begins with "Well, I…," we have immediately answered wrong; our answer can begin with only one word: "Jesus…" It is what Jesus did for us on the cross and not anything else that allows us into heaven. Neither our good works nor our fine words can save us; only what Jesus the Anointed One achieved on His cross can rescue us from eternal sin and death.

Jesus was authoritatively adamant in His promise to the thief, with a definite deadline in mind. He spoke from a platform of Truth. He assured the man that what He said was true, and He promised it would happen "today." It was late morning, almost noon, when Jesus made this promise. In the Jewish mindset, the day would be over in little more than six hours. "When next we talk *today,* just a few hours

---

1 Begg, A. (2022, June 28). "The man on the middle cross said I can come." Blog Archive of Truth For Life with Alistair Begg for: /. https://blog.truthforlife.org/the-man-on-the-middle-cross-said-i-can-come#fn1

from now, you *will* be with me in paradise." If the thief could have even begun to comprehend what Jesus meant by this, his heart must have leapt in his chest! He had only a glimmer of Who Christ was – he knew He had never done anything wrong – but that was enough.

The only exception I will take with Mr. Begg's brilliant tongue-in-cheek commentary is this: I know the angels would not have dared to engage the criminal in Begg's witty repartee. How can I be so sure of this? Because Jesus promised, "Today, you will be *with **Me*** in Paradise!" He *Himself* escorted the thief into Paradise, into Sheol, into Abraham's bosom later that very day, right after He finished speaking His final Word from His cross. Jesus' angels would *never* question Him on any point. Jesus ushered His fellow "insurrectionist" into Paradise with all the pomp and circumstance that He Himself might have been accorded. What a promise! What a joy!

Provision for His Mother
"Woman, look upon your son… look upon your mother."

Following His exchange with the thief, His mother Mary pressed forward to be near Him, supported by John the Beloved and by her sister Salome. Mary Alphaeus (wife of Clopas Alphaeus and mother of James Alphaeus), and Mary of Magdala were also there. Helpless to serve Him in any way other than only to be there with Him in His agony, their five weeping faces merely stared up at him from the crowd.

There, with all the sins of the world upon Him mingling with His draining blood and dwindling breath, Jesus somehow gathered the strength to provide for His widowed mother. As her oldest son, this was His responsibility. His eldest half-brother, her next eldest son, James, was not there: in fact, there is evidence to suggest that His half-brothers and sisters did not acquire saving faith in Him until after His resurrection, despite the fact that James would become the first pastor of the Jerusalem Church. More on that later.

Here indeed, however, did stand His cousin and beloved disciple John. Probably one of the youngest of the disciples, he would certainly be able to care for Mary until her demise. Likely yet unmarried, John may still have been living at home with Zebedee and Salome so taking Mary into his home would have been bringing her into her sister and brother-in-law's home as well, a ready-made, already-familiar family, including John's brother James. Jesus' care for His mother was perfect and His love for John was perfect, as were all His deeds on that side of His grave.

I should hasten to point out that Jesus meant no disrespect to His dear mother when He called her, "Woman." Indeed, at the wedding feast of Cana, when Mary had approached Jesus about the need for more wine, He replied in John 2:4, "Dear woman, why do you involve me?... My time has not yet come" Mary seemingly ignores Him and told the servants, "Do whatever He tells you." This is the playful repartee of a knowing relationship between mother and son. Further, Mary is not the only female with whom Jesus uses this word. There are cultural differences also, as one might well imagine, between New Testament Greek and contemporary American English. The Greek word for "woman," *gynai*, from which we get our word *gynecology* and its derivatives, seems to have carried a connotation very similar to our *ma'am* today.

THE EIGHT *FIRST* WORDS OF CHRIST

I must explain my translation of this saying – "Woman, look upon your son… look upon your mother" and point out the double entendre of another word in these verses. The Greek word *ide* occurs thirty-four times in Scripture and is most commonly translated as *behold*; however, the English word *behold* has fallen quite out of favor in contemporary American usage which is why I chose the wording *look upon* above. Other translations use "here is your son…here is your mother," but that does not seem to utilize the sense of sight, with *see* or *look* being the other most common translations of *ide*. There is an intimacy in a mother/son relationship from birth that involves the eyes. How many of us have heard our mothers say to us, "Look at me" when she had something important to say? In saying, "Woman, look upon your son," Jesus is not only asking her to look at Him one last time, painful though it be, that He might look into her eyes with all of His love for her; but also to look upon her nephew and His best friend John with favor as His successor in caring for her.

To John, no appellation is necessary; the thought follows naturally: "look upon your mother." Nothing more is needed between the older and younger cousins, between the Teacher and His disciple, between the Master and His bondservant, between the King and His prime minister, between Jesus and His beloved friend. The unspoken thoughts between them: *look upon her, look after her, take care of her, be all that I would be to and for her into her dotage and until her passing.* What a loving son! What a caring Savior!

A Son's Cry of Separation from His Father
"Eloi, Eloi, lama sabachthani?" "My God, my God, why have You forsaken Me?"

Then, at high noon, when the sun should have been at its highest, darkness fell over the hill, the city, and all of Israel. Luke goes so far as to say that the sun stopped shining altogether. Certainly, there was a thick cover of clouds. It was a surreal darkness, an other-worldly night in the middle of the day. Imagine: birdsong ceased immediately, and night creatures only gradually stirred. The temperature drop was precipitous, especially for the men hanging naked on their crosses. Fear fell upon all humanity, and words would have been hushed if spoken at all. Absent sun, absent light, absent warmth, absent sound, and absent… God.

This was the moment when God turned His back on the sins of the world, despite the fact that they were all laid upon His only begotten Son. Imagine the pain of that realization for Jesus! The Godhood of which Jesus had emptied Himself to walk among people, first as a baby, then a child, then a servant, to humble Himself and become obedient to this very end, death on a cross (Philippians 2:7-8) – that God had abandoned Him.

The Father Who had sired Him in a virgin womb and knit Him together in that secret place, making Him fearfully and wonderfully, seeing His unformed body formed just like they had together made the world out of nothing in the beginning, "all the days ordained for Me were written in Your book before one of them came to be" (Psalm 139:13-16): that Father's hands had abandoned Him.

The Father Whom the Son had sought out day after day after day in prayer, in solitude, in lonely places, in deserts, on mountains, by the lake, far from the madding crowd: that Father was nowhere near this lonely cross.

The Father Who had given Him every Word to speak and the power to drive out demons and heal all manner of sickness and disease – that Father was silent, non-exorcising, unhealing! He had never before personally experienced this kind of absence and loss. The pain was even greater than when his stepfather, Joseph, had died. God's absence was greater than He could bear. Jesus wept.

It took His breath away and left Him speechless for three hours! At about 3:00 in the afternoon, however, Jesus rallied his strength and loudly cried out in Hebrew, "*Eloi, Eloi, lama sabachthani?*" Despite the volume and repetition of His cry, some of those still standing there misunderstood Him to be calling for Elijah instead. Perhaps to help Him clear His throat and get more clarity but certainly not out of compassion or any kindness, one man immediately filled a sponge with the Roman soldiers' *posca,* a mixture of water and wine vinegar, without the bitter analgesic of gall and myrrh which they'd offered to him initially. He stuck the sponge on a stick and shoved it up for Jesus to drink. Then he and the rest of the group continued to mock: "Now leave Him alone, and we'll see if Elijah will take Him down and save Him or not."

His was the cry of a child separated from His parents, lost in the marketplace, desperate to be back safe in the strong arms of His father, showered with His mother's tears of relief. This was not the twelve-year-old Jesus, confident in His newfound coming of age and anxious to be about His heavenly Father's business in the Temple. This was not the thirty-year-old Jesus, exhausted from battling temptation in the wilderness and merely desirous of angel ministrations – only the Father would do in this moment. This was the cry of abandonment. This was not only Paradise Lost, but Jesus Lost. Alone. For the first time ever, the Son was separated from His Father.

Notice, however, that it is not only the Father to Whom He makes His cry: it is to the Triune God. In these hours on the cross, His own Spirit has abandoned Him. His mind, soul, and body would be His until His final breath; but the Dove that had descended upon Him at His baptism was nowhere to be seen among the crows and ravens drawn to the blood and the carrion raptors circling overhead. That inner voice Who all through His earthly journey had constantly been speaking, "This Is the way. Walk In It." had fallen silent.

With Father and Spirit so obviously absent, what was the Son without them? In these dark, God-forsaken hours, the absence of the sun could only reflect the absence of the Son as well; for what power could the Son exercise without the Trinity? Even as His detractors had taunted Him, could He even, in those dark hours, have accomplished what He claimed during His arrest in the Garden? In the dark abandonment of His soul, without His Father and Holy Spirit, could He have *then* made good His boast to summon twelve legions of angels to rescue Him (Matt. 26:53)?

It is remarkable that, the moment Jesus managed to cry out to His God, the darkness lifted. I have to believe the Father immediately not only heard His Son's heartbroken and heartbreaking cry but also turned His face back to Him to prove He had *not*, indeed, forsaken Him. He immediately answered His Son's prayer with *light*, and the darkness had to flee in both thought and in reality.

It is important to note that both Matthew and Mark felt the imperative to translate the Aramaic Hebrew into Greek to make sure both Jew and Gentile knew the meaning of Christ's fourth "last" word on the cross. Both the Aramaic and the Greek translate to the English, "My God, my God, why have You forsaken Me?" This feeling of abandonment by God is a universal part of the human condition because sin always separates us from God, and "all have sinned and fall short of God's glory (Rom. 3:23)"; and it's important to know that Christ, even though He Himself was sinless, can identify in this pain of separation from God.

Some have suggested that, although only the first half of the first verse of Psalm 22 is recorded, Jesus actually may have quoted the entire psalm after the sponge had been thrust in His face. The psalm is obviously Messianic in tone and nature, but that even Jesus would have had strength for so Aristotelian a task as quoting what amounts to thirty-one verses in our Bible translations while in the final throes of death is specious at best and doubtful at least. Suffice that He at least directed our attention to the psalm of His father David; I commend you to its reading.

An Acknowledgement of Thirst
"I thirst."

Somehow, He knew. Perhaps it was the sun shining down on Him again, that symbol that God had heard His desperate cry. Perhaps He knew He had lost sufficient blood. Perhaps it was merely a lingering drop of *posca* from when the man had earlier shoved a warm, dripping sponge in His face; but He *knew* His trial and suffering in this world was coming to a rapid end. It is possible that somewhere in the dim reaches of His God-Mind, He had an inkling, a distant and niggling memory of Psalm 69:21 and knew that He had eventually to accept the wine vinegar they had offered him twice; but I think His human mind was much more in control when He said, "*Dipso.* I thirst." Jesus was parched! Psalm 22:15a & b says, "my strength is dried up like a potsherd, and my tongue sticks to my jaws...," an apt description of a crucified man who has lost so much blood and water and hasn't had a drink since *before* He offered the final cups to His apostles some nineteen hours earlier, when He'd said, "I will not drink from the fruit of the vine again until God's Kingdom comes." "I thirst" was the understatement of all time!

Notice that there is no hesitation in fulfilling His request. "They" were likely the soldiers who had overseen His crucifixion; and after an afternoon of unnatural darkness, they were not likely still eager to prolong His suffering and death. More perfunctorily than His earlier persecutors who had mocked Him by offering a drink, the soldiers soaked a sea sponge in *posca*, again without the gall and myrrh, speared it on a stalk of "hyssop" (likely "Bible hyssop", which is Syrian Oregano, rather than *Hyssopus officinalis*), and gave it to Jesus, Who drank it because He wanted to and needed to, primarily to relieve legitimate thirst but also to fulfill Psalm 69:21: "They put gall in my food and gave me vinegar for my thirst" (*NIV*).

These final three "last words" of Christ happened in relatively rapid succession after 3:00 in the afternoon. That Jesus died shortly after 3:00 is important to the narrative of all else that had to be accomplished before sundown that day, which marked the beginning of the Jewish sabbath. That "I thirst" is the fifth "last word" is indubitable, but the ordering of the final two sayings of Christ appears to be debatable.

THE EIGHT *FIRST* WORDS OF CHRIST

Descriptions of death immediately follow each account, one in Luke 23:46 and one in John 19:30. I have decided to go with what I believe is the natural progress of human death, the louder commitment preceding what is apparently a quieter assent to death's reality. Still, there was nothing "natural" about Christ's life or death so, if someone thinks differently on these matters, I will not argue the point.

A Cry of Resignation
"Father, into Your hands, I commit my spirit."

His voice strengthened and cleared by the mixture of water and sour wine vinegar, Jesus called out with a loud voice for all within range to hear, "Father, into Your hands, I commit My Spirit." The Trinity – Father, Son, and Holy Spirit – is reunited at last, if only for a moment! Jesus is recommitting to the unity of the Godhead in that moment in preparation for His exaltation to come. Having "emptied Himself" and become "obedient to the point of death, even death on a cross," He will soon refill Himself with His Godhead and take His rightful place at the right hand of His Father in Heaven (Phil. 2:5-11).

Despite the abandonment He had felt earlier, Jesus knew He could commit His spirit, even His Holy Spirit, into His Father's hands, and could know that God would keep it safe for Him until He would be reunited with it in His resurrection. Although He had emptied Himself of His Godhead before entering this world as a fertilized egg in Mary's womb, Jesus in His humanity came to understand so much about His Heavenly Father; and He knew above all He could be trusted. Father knows best!

It is important to recognize that Jesus did not cry out with a loud voice in order for the Father to hear Him: God could have heard a whisper, even a thought. I am reminded of Jesus at Lazarus' graveside and His words, "Father, I thank you that you have heard me. I knew that you always hear me, but I said this on account of the people standing around, that they may believe that you sent me (John 11:41b-42)."

It's equally important, however, that Christ *could* cry out with a loud voice. He had *willingly* laid down His life for us. Jesus did not die from a position of weakness but a position of strength. "For this reason the Father loves me because I lay down my life that I may take it up again. No one takes it from me, but I lay it down of my own accord. I have authority to lay it down, and I have authority to take it up again. This charge I have received from my Father (John 10:17-18)."

Because Jesus' cry here is actually a quote of Psalm 31:5, we would do well to look at it in its entirety. The second half of the verse says, "You have redeemed me, O Lord, faithful God." Even while He was in the end throes of death, Jesus was counting on His Father to save Him, to redeem Him from death and the grave. As Jesus' life blood drained from His body, there was no doubt that the plan, now well in motion and about to reach both its apex and its lowest moment, would succeed. Jesus knew He could trust God because He is a faithful God and His redemption on the other side of this death was secure.

Luke states, "And having said this, He breathed His last"; but we will let John the Beloved have the final Word.

THE EIGHT *FIRST* WORDS OF CHRIST

A Sigh of Accomplishment
"It is finished"

The exertion of His loud commitment of His spirit into His Father's hand left Him exhausted as He hung limply on the bloody cross. His head swam in and out of consciousness. His lips were again dry, and His mouth and tongue were beginning to dry as well. He opened His eye: John and the women still wept at His feet. It was time to put an end to their suffering. He had done all He could do. He knew He had accomplished the work that He and His Father and His Holy Spirit had set out to do.

"It is finished." Done. God's Kingdom had come; God's will had been done on earth just as He had planned it in heaven. Every Word the Father had given Him to say, He had passed on to both His disciples – from "Follow me" and "Look upon your mother" – and His enemies – from the first cleansing of the Temple to "You would have no power over me if were not given to you from above; therefore, the one who handed me over to you is guilty of a greater sin." His teaching duties were discharged. Every miracle the Father had given Him to do, from turning the water to wine in Cana to raising Lazarus from death (oh, and that stray withering of the fig tree that week) had been accomplished. From the long-distance healing of the royal official's boy in Capernaum whom He had healed while in Cana to the healing of Malchus' ear the night of His arrest in Gethsemane, every healing had been realized. The only sinless, blameless, spotless man to have ever lived had been slain for the sins of the whole world, past, present, and future. "Behold the Lamb of God, Who takes away the sins of the world." The sacrifice was complete. "For God so loved the world, that He gave His only Son, that whoever believes in Him should not perish but have eternal life." This battle was over.

"'It is finished.' With that, He bowed His head and gave up His spirit." Death didn't take it from Him. Even at the very last, He *willingly* laid down His life for us.

Thus ends the seven last words of Christ from the cross....

THE EIGHT *FIRST* WORDS OF CHRIST

For Further Contemplation and Discussion:

Prior to this study, what was your exposure to the seven last words of Christ from the cross?

If you have heard them before, what new insights did you gain from this chapter?

If this is your first time hearing of them, what significance did you find in them?

Did you have any fresh insights into the narrative of the story of Jesus' crucifixion?

Which of the seven last sayings of Christ means the most to you? Why?

THE EIGHT *FIRST* WORDS OF CHRIST

CHAPTER TWO

The Eight First Words of Christ: An Overview

When trying to determine the words that Jesus spoke from the time He exited the tomb to His ascension into heaven, I first turned to A. T. Robertson's *A Harmony of the Gospels: The Standard Broadus Harmony thoroughly Revised, Rearranged, and Enlarged* as well as Thomas and Gundry's harmony of the *New International Version*. For those unfamiliar with the term, a *harmony* of the gospels is an attempt to place the good news of Jesus Christ – his birth, childhood, baptism, temptation, life, ministry, teachings, miracles, trials, death, burial, resurrection, appearances, and ascension – as told by the four gospel authors and a few references from Acts and the Apostles' epistles – into a chronological order. Just as the seven *last* words of Christ from the cross are studied in chronological order, so I want to look at the eight *first* words of Christ out of the tomb.

My first order of business was to list the appearances of Jesus following his resurrection in chronological order, identifying those in which I knew He said something.

THE EIGHT *FIRST* WORDS OF CHRIST

He appeared and spoke first to Mary Magdalene (John 20:14 & Mark 16:9) and then to the other women as they headed back from the tomb (Matthew 28:9). He next appeared to Peter (Luke 24:34 & I Corinthians 15:5), but we have no record of their exchange. He then appeared for a lengthy conversation with Cleopas and another disciple on the road to and in Emmaus (Luke 24:13-35), giving them just enough time to return to the tell the other disciples before appearing to the entire group, sans Thomas, behind locked doors to finish out His first day out of the tomb (Mark 16:4, Luke 24:36, & John 20:19). Eight days later, he appeared to the disciples again in their meeting place in Jerusalem, this time with Thomas present (John 20:26*ff*). Eventually, the appearances and conversations migrated north to the region of Galilee, where He appeared again to seven of the disciples while they were out fishing (John 21:1-24) and had an extended conversation with Peter after breakfast. Next, he appeared to the Eleven (and apparently over 500 other disciples; see I Corinthians 15:6) on a mountain in Galilee, during which He gave what we have come to know as The Great Commission (Matthew 28:16*ff* & Mark 16:15*ff*). He appeared to his eldest half-brother James, but the words that brought James to faith in His big brother as His Lord and Savior are not recorded (I Corinthians 15:7a). He also appeared to *all* the "apostles," and I later came to believe we do have a record of that exchange. Then He appeared to the Eleven and another large group back in Jerusalem in which he gave them instructions to wait in Jerusalem until they had received the gift of the Holy Spirit and continued instructions for their mission (Luke 24:50*ff* & Acts 1:3-12). Finally, notice that all of Jesus post-resurrection appearances were to His disciples, His followers, those who had some modicum of belief or at least very good reason to believe in Him. The possible exception to this might be His half-brother James. He didn't appear to Saul, another unbeliever at the time, until *after* His ascension into heaven.

To return to the Story, we'll return to John's relation of events since he is the only one to tell this next part. "'It is finished.' With that, He bowed His head and gave up His spirit." Death didn't take it from Him. Even at the very last, He *willingly* laid down His life for us. Jesus' body is hanging lifelessly on the "tree."

The chief priests, scribes, and elders had not hung around to see Jesus' demise. Likely spooked by the ongoing mid-day darkness and its portent, they had headed back to Pilate to hasten the demise of the three Jews on the hill. Ever focused on keeping the minutiae of the Law, they were concerned that the next day, which would begin at sundown, was a particularly high and holy Sabbath for them. Deuteronomy 21:22-23 forbade dead bodies to be left impaled on "a tree" overnight, any night, but especially on a holy Sabbath: it was curse enough in God's eyes that a man had been crucified; he was to be buried the same day he died. The Jews therefore asked that Pilate have the three insurrectionists' legs broken. This would prevent them from pushing up from their feet to fill their lungs with air, and they would die sooner rather than later.

Pilate sent a currier to the cross to instruct the centurion to fulfill the Jews' request. The soldiers carried out the edict, breaking the legs of the first thief and then the second; but when they came to Jesus on the middle cross, they discovered He was already dead. Instead of breaking His legs, one of the soldiers pierced Jesus' side with a spear, bursting His pericardium and releasing a gush of blood and water, demonstrating that He had indeed already passed and His bodily fluids had already begun to separate. John the Beloved, writing some sixty years after the actual events, says in 19:36-37, "For these things took place that the Scripture might be fulfilled: 'Not one of his bones will be broken [Psalm 34:20].' And again another Scripture says, 'They will look on him whom they have pierced [Zechariah 12:10].'"

The chief priests, scribes, and elders, however, were not the only Jews concerned with removing Jesus from the disgraceful cross and burying His body before the high, holy Sabbath began. Two wealthy Jews, Joseph from the town of Arimathea in the former territory of Ephraim in Israel, and Nicodemus ben Gurion, the same man who had approached Jesus under cover of darkness to discover Who He truly was in John 3, were both members of the Sanhedrin, the ruling body of seventy elders over the Temple. These two had voted *against* Jesus' crucifixion to no avail and were both followers of Jesus in secret because they feared their murderous colleagues. Joseph and Nicodemus took it upon themselves to request Jesus' body from Pilate in order to bury Him. Since it was the responsibility of the father or oldest living relative to claim a crucified body and because Jesus' stepfather, Joseph, had already passed, some scholars have conjectured that Joseph of Arimathea was Mary's uncle and saw it as his responsibility to claim the body; but it could also have easily been, as a loving though secret follower of Jesus and having so recently carved out his own tomb so near the site of the crucifixion, that it merely made sense to Joseph to beg the body boldly from Pilate, given his position and means. Mark tells us that

Pilate was surprised to learn that Jesus was already dead so he summoned the centurion to verify the death. When he learned it was true, he gave Joseph permission to collect and bury the body.

Joseph provided a large, clean linen cloth in which to wrap the body, and Nicodemus brought a hundred (Roman) pounds (seventy-five American pounds) of mixed myrrh and aloe, two ground, spicy, odiferous resins to place between strips of linen to wrap the draped body. It is interesting to note that Jesus was wrapped in strips of linen cloth in His death in the same way as he was swaddled and laid in the manger as an infant: "Naked I came from my mother's womb, and naked shall I return. The LORD gave, and the LORD has taken away; blessed be the name of the LORD (Job 1:21)." It is equally interesting that His future wedding clothes as described in the Royal Wedding Psalm 45:8 are scented with the same fragrances: "your robes are all fragrant with myrrh and aloes and cassia."

There is no reason to believe that these two wealthy men struggled with Jesus' body at all: as wealthy men, they had an entourage of servants to assist them in getting the body from the cross to the tomb, wrapped in the spices and laid to rest well before the sun went down. The women wisely watched to see where the tomb was so they could return on the day after the Sabbath, more properly to spice and perfume the body. Once Jesus' body was laid to rest, they all went home.

The next evening, our Saturday evening, the moment the high, holy Sabbath ended found the chief priests and Pharisees back on Pilate's doorstep: "Sir, it crosses our minds that, while he was still alive, that trickster said, 'After three days, I will rise again.' Please command soldiers to secure the tomb until Monday evening so his disciples can't come and steal the body and tell people he was raised from the dead. That sort of deceit would be worse than all his other fraudulence combined."

Pilate answered them: "Take a guard. Go, make the tomb secure to your exacting satisfaction." They did so, placing a seal on the stone and posting a guard of Roman soldiers.

The day dawned as what we celebrate today as Easter or Resurrection Sunday morning. The soldiers had spent a quiet night guarding the tomb; and the women rose early from their beds, gathering their spices and perfumes and a lantern or torch or two to make their way through the early morning darkness out to Jesus' tomb. Suddenly, there was a violent earthquake because an angel of the Lord came down from heaven, rolled back the stone, opening the grave, and sat on what had been the stone door. He was so bright and his clothes so white that even the battle-seasoned Roman guards shook in fear and fainted away like dead men. When they revived, they ran away before the women arrived. They knew they were dead men walking because they had failed to keep the tomb sealed, even though the "thief" was God Himself!

Piecing together the various narratives, it was Mary Magdalene, Mary Alphaeus, Salome, Joanna (wife of Chuza, Herod's household manager), and at least one other woman (Susanna is the only other name we have in Scripture besides Jesus' mother Mary) who made their way to the tomb that morning. As they walked, they wondered among themselves, "Who will roll the stone away from the entrance of the tomb?" They had heard nothing of the posted guard the night before and had not thought to look for some of the men to come with them, but they had seen Joseph and Nicodemus' servants settle the stone in place with a resounding thud on Friday evening.

As they came in sight of the tomb, they were surprised to find the stone had been rolled away already! When they entered the tomb, the first thing they noticed, or rather didn't see, was Jesus' body. It was gone! Mary Magdalene was the first to respond. Immediately believing someone had moved the body, she bolted from the tomb and ran to find Peter and John!

No sooner had Maggie gone than two angels, bright as lightning, appeared to stand by the remaining four ladies (probably in case they fainted) and a third angel, who looked like a young man, sat on the right side of the tomb. The women were so frightened, they fell with their faces to the ground, but the seated angel spoke: "Don't be alarmed! You are looking for Jesus of Nazareth who was crucified, but why are you looking for the living where only the dead should be? He has risen! He is not here. See: that's the stone table where they laid His body. Remember how He told you while He was still with you in Galilee: 'The Son of Man must be delivered to sinful men to be crucified and on the third day be raised again?'"

The women blinked at one another, remembering those very words.

"Now go, tell His disciples, especially Peter: Jesus is going ahead of you into Galilee. You will see Him there just as He promised."

Shaken and confused, the four ladies fled, afraid at first to tell a single soul.

In the meantime, Maggie, still panicked, found Peter and John the Beloved, who were perhaps on the way to the tomb themselves to help the women. "They've taken my Lord out of the tomb, and we don't know where they've put Him!" she blurted out. Peter and John took one look at each other and took off running to the tomb. John, being younger and the better runner, got there first but merely stooped over to look in. Peter, however, arrived and characteristically dove in, followed by John. They found the grave clothes empty and lying flat and the bandana that had covered Jesus' face folded neatly and laid to the side. Peter went away wondering, and John went away believing, even though they still didn't understand that Jesus had to rise from the dead.

For Further Contemplation and Discussion:

What additional hypocrisy of the Jewish Sanhedrin especially strikes you when you consider Christ's trials and crucifixion?

The number of Old Testament prophesies fulfilled in the crucifixion alone is astounding. Read Psalm 22. Count the number of ways Jesus fulfilled this psalm alone on the cross.

THE EIGHT *FIRST* WORDS OF CHRIST

How many angels were at the tomb? Matthew says one angel rolled away the stone and stuck around to talk to the ladies. Mark says, "a young man in a white robe was *sitting* on the right side" while Luke says, "two men in clothes that gleamed like lightning *stood* beside them." Does it matter?

Why do you think it was especially important to God for Peter to hear that Jesus was planning to meet them in Galilee?

CHAPTER THREE

Word One
"Woman, why are you weeping? ... Whom are you seeking? ... Mary…"

Mary just stood in the road, dumbfounded. Not a word. They'd just run off! *Men.* She could do nothing but hurry back after them. She found herself exhausted, the adrenaline spent in her effort to get to Peter and John in the first place. Her lungs were heaving and her head, swimming. *They've taken away my Lord, and we don't know where they've put Him.* Over and over, the message pounded away in her mind. *I've got to find Him. I must save Him from them.*

As she hastened to the tomb, she realized she didn't even know who she thought "they" were. Had the Romans removed the body? They preferred to leave the bodies on the crosses until the sun and elements had done their damage and the birds had picked clean the flesh. The crucified were not worthy of burial in their minds. Had the Jewish religious leaders exhumed the corpse? After all, Joseph and Nicodemus were members of the Sanhedrin. Perhaps they themselves had thought better of their generosity and moved the body to a less conspicuous tomb, one not so closely associated with Joseph. Could some other of the disciples have moved Him? Peter and John certainly gave no indication in the split second before they ran off that they knew anything about it, but the Master had many, many followers beyond the Twelve and their intimate circle. Could some other disciple have stolen the body to venerate it elsewhere? Her mind ricocheted from one thought to the next. Her one settled thought: He was her Master even in death, and she *would* know what had happened.

She neared the tomb now again. There was no sign of Peter or John, which pulled her up short and stirred her fear. "Peter? John?" Her tentative voice dampened by the morning mist, the silence echoed in the rising sun. "Peter! John!" she cried out, believing her thoughts could not have dragged her so far behind them for them to have gotten too far away. Apart from morning birdsong, the silence remained. Mary could go no further. Overwhelmed by fear and anxiety, the dam burst; and she sobbed freely while standing in front of the grave.

As she wept, she leaned over to look into the tomb, which was slowly being illuminated by the sun rising behind her, casting her shadow long into the tomb. There, shimmering through her tears, she saw two men dressed in white, one sitting at the head and one at the foot of the table upon which Jesus' body had lain. She assumed they were angels, which startled her. One addressed her kindly, "Woman…" and the other asked, "Why are you weeping?"

"They have taken my Lord away, and I don't know where they've put him," she sobbed. She was ugly crying and didn't care. She thought she saw the face of the angel nearest her brighten in recognition at something or someone behind her so she turned, shielding her still-weeping eyes from the rising sun. She saw Jesus Himself standing there; but with the sun, her tears, and her lack of expectation, she didn't recognize Him.

Before we get too far away from them, I want to point out something unusual about the angels in this encounter. If we carefully analyze every human interaction with angels in Scripture, we will see one aspect that every single instance has in common: angels *always* deliver a message from God. It's in their DNA, if angels have DNA. If they're not delivering a message, they're protecting people, battling evil, or worshiping and praising God. Since they're not doing the latter three, they must have been sent to deliver a message, but apparently their Supervisor Himself interrupted their mission because He wanted to deliver this one personally. How Jesus must have loved Mary!

Here it is, the *first* first word or saying of Christ, literally just outside His tomb: "Woman, why are you weeping? Whom are you seeking?" Notice that his first question is exactly the same question His angels had just asked. This is one reason I believe He was merely continuing the message the angels were sent to give; but note, too, the nature of the question. "Woman, why are you weeping." This is Jesus' first attempt after His resurrection to "wipe every tear from our eyes (Rev. 21:4)." Secondly, He asks "Whom are you seeking." Look at what presumably these same two angels had said earlier to the other women whom Mary left at the tomb in her haste to find Peter and John. In every synoptic gospel, we find, after addressing their fear, these angels addressed the ladies' search: "…I know that you seek Jesus who was crucified (Matt. 28:5)," "You seek Jesus of Nazareth, who was crucified (Mark 16:6)," and "Why do you seek the living among the dead (Luke 24:5)?" These angels' message to Mary would have been the same as to her friends, but Jesus Himself intervened, in order to deliver the same information Himself, with His personal spin on it.

It is interesting that the angels, appearing to the other women earlier, knew whom they were seeking and why; but Jesus, here with Mary, chooses to "play dumb": "Whom are you seeking?" It is often said that God wants us to "let our requests be made known unto Him" not because He doesn't already know everything we want or need but because we need to hear ourselves ask and learn more about ourselves. What might Mary have learned from her answer to Jesus' question?

Again, tears and sun in her eyes and no expectation of seeing her crucified Lord alive, Mary assumes He is the gardener. Who else would be in a garden just as the sun was coming up on the very first day of the week? Certainly not the blue-blood garden owner or his wife! And how long might he have been standing there? Surely the guys in the tomb were not gardeners, dressed in white as they were. She might have assumed He'd been there long enough to hear her response to those two concerning the reason for her tears; regardless, she did not dignify His question about her tears with a response. She simply plunged on, bent upon her quest. "Sir, if you have carried him away, tell me where you have laid him, and I will take him away." Really, Mary? And how do you propose to do that? You singlehandedly are going to carry a full-grown dead man wrapped in cloth and holding at least fifty pounds of spices in those bandages from wherever He is now to wherever you are going to put him to rest, which, by the way, is where? Oh, my dear, Mary, Mary, Mary…

"Mary." Her name washed over her like a wave of immediate relief: not cold, bracing water like a slap in the face; but warm, tension-shooing relief came over her from head to toe. Never had her name sounded so beautifully in her ear. Her mere name, filled with so much love, identification, and passion that it could only have been spoken in one way by One Person. Not only was she known and seen, but she *knew and saw* the One who spoke her name. As distinguished British theologian Charles Ellicott wrote in 1878, "The voice of God is always most quickly heard by the hearts that love Him; the presence of God is never so truly felt as in the utter helplessness of human woe."

"Rabboni!" John the Beloved so quickly translates the Aramaic Hebrew to "teacher" in the Greek; but oh, so accustomed was John to his own Hebrew mind that he fell short in communicating to a modern American culture the honor Mary intended in that one word. The Aramaic title *Rab* meant simply a "Master"; *Rabbi* meant "*my* Master", and *Rabboni* meant 'my *great and most honorable of all* Masters. This third title historically has only been conferred on seven other Jewish men. The Galilean dialect would have heard "*Rabbouni.*" Blind Bartimaeus also uses this term in Mark 10:51 when He asks Jesus for his sight.

Upon recognizing Him, Mary immediately fell prostrate at Jesus' feet, perhaps grasping them or His ankles. Jesus said to her, "Do not cling to me, for I have not yet ascended to the Father." I don't think Jesus was expressing any concern that somehow, any moment, His Father might snatch Him up to heaven and Mary would be

THE EIGHT *FIRST* WORDS OF CHRIST

caught dangling dangerously from His feet; rather, Jesus was gently letting her know there would be another time for pleasantries, that He wasn't flying off to heaven just yet. They would have time together; but for the moment both of them had work to do.

"…But go to my brothers and say to them, 'I am ascending to my Father and your Father, to my God and your God." Jesus needed Mary to testify of His resurrection to His "brothers." They began as mere followers and then had become His servants. They then became His students, His disciples; and just before His death, in the upper room, He had called them His friends; but now, although these same men had denied, forsaken, and run from Him – one even left his clothes in a soldier's hand and fled naked into the night! – still He called them His *brothers*. They only had a little time left (forty days, but how they would fly by!) before Father would call Him to come Home.

Jesus reached down and helped Mary to her feet, perhaps just as He had after the seven demons left her for dead and for good. Her tears of anxiety and fear had changed to tears of joy and relief. She quickly assented to her Lord's request and, rejuvenated, ran off to tell the disciples the good news, the tears still streaming down her face, laughing like a schoolgirl!

For Further Contemplation and Discussion:

Jesus "played dumb" in asking whom she was seeking. What do you think He might have wanted Mary to learn in her request to find her Lord?

Why do you think Jesus may have interrupted His angels' message to Mary and chosen to deliver it Himself?

THE EIGHT *FIRST* WORDS OF CHRIST

I find it interesting that the very first person to whom Jesus both appeared and spoke was Mary Magdalene, a woman and not His mother or one of His half-sisters. Why a woman? Why Mary? Why not His mother?

Consider the "dramatic" value of these "First Words of Christ Out the Tomb." Imagine yourself suddenly confronted by Jesus when you thought He was dead. How might you respond? What questions would you ask? What might He say to you?

CHAPTER FOUR

Word Two
"Fear not!"

When they had run far enough to be sure the angels weren't following them, Susannah and Joanna slowed down to let the two older women, Salome and Mary Alphaeus, catch up. They stopped to catch their breath and looked at one another incredulously, eyes wide, unsure of what even to say to one another. Suddenly, they all started talking at once:

"What was that?"

"Were those angels?"

"Where's Mary?"

"I'm right here."

"No, the Magdalene…"

"That light was so bright, I still can't see well!"

"Did he say Jesus is risen? What does that even mean?"

"Remember? He said that to us once in Galilee, but I didn't think…"

"Did you see? I think those were the grave clothes lying flat on the table…"

THE EIGHT *FIRST* WORDS OF CHRIST

"Dare we hope?"

"Dare we believe?"

"Dare we go tell the others and appear to be babbling idiots?" Susanna was close to tears.

Salome was the first to sniff up her nose and collect their thoughts, "Well, I can tell you my James and John had better not think their own mother a babbling idiot! Zebedee won't allow it!"

"Same with my James. Clopas would have his hide!" Mary replied, smiling weakly.

Always practical, Joanna brought them back to reality. "Until Friday, Jesus was a mere curiosity to Herod, but Chuza says Herod's been troubled ever since he mocked Him and sent Him back to Pilate on Friday morning. Herod already thought that Jesus might have been the Baptizer raised from the dead. If now He really *has* risen from the dead Himself...." Joanna shuddered at the potential implications.

"But He *did* tell us He was going to Jerusalem to be crucified and that He would be raised again on the third day!" Susanna was still puzzling over how not to sound like a babbling idiot when they told the others. All the women did the mental math along with her: "Let's see... Joseph and Nicodemus laid him in the tomb late Friday afternoon, and He's been there through the entire sabbath, and today would be the third day..." The other women stared at her, each one slowly nodding her head in agreement. Together, they slowly inhaled then exhaled a collective sigh.

Salome broke the silence. "Well, then, I suppose we should go get this message to the menfolk."

"Especially Peter, they said," Susanna quickly added.

"Let's get our story straight first," Salome continued, "Mary, what did you hear?"

Mary Alphaeus replied, "Jesus is going ahead of us into Galilee, and we're to meet Him there."

Joanna quoted the angel exactly: "You will see Him there just as He promised."

"That's what I said," replied Mary.

"Okay, then," Salome dabbed her forehead and eyes with her veil and then tucked in a few stray hairs and smoothed it over her head. "I don't think there's any need to run like the demons of hell are after us, but let's go deliver this –"

Out of nowhere, the Magdalene burst past them running on the road! Realizing it was them, she stopped and wheeled on them. "Come on! I've just seen Jesus, and He's alive! We've got to go tell the others!" she shouted and turned on her heels toward town. The other four women took off after her at breakneck speed. As they rounded the bend to head into the city, suddenly Jesus met them.

"Greetings and salutations!" He called out, stopping them dead in their tracks. Their collective gasp removed all the oxygen in the air for a quarter of a mile! They ran to Him, and all five women fell at His feet, grabbing his feet, ankles, and legs, threatening to send Him sprawling. He laughed. "Fear not! Go and tell my brothers to go to Galilee, and there they will see me."

The women choked, sobbed, mumbled, blurted and chortled, "Yes, Master. Of course, Master. Yes, that's just what we were about to… just what we were on our way to do, yes, yes, we were" as they scrambled to their feet, straightened their clothing, and bowed and clasped their hands over their hearts before Him.

THE EIGHT *FIRST* WORDS OF CHRIST

"Come on!" the Magdalene shouted, and loath to turn and leave him, they all ran off to deliver His message.

Arriving at the home of Mary Marcus and her Roman husband, the women gamboled into the courtyard, absolutely giddy with the excitement of their news. Surprisingly, someone had left the door unlocked. At the sound of the commotion, everyone came running into the courtyard. Salome ran to her son James and asked after John, whom James had not seen since early this morning. Zebedee hurried up behind them. Mary kissed Clopas Alphaeus on the lips, shocking their son James and prompting a hushed "Motherrrr…." Susanna and Joanna quickly grabbed the hands of their hostess Mary Marcus and her son John to be sure they heard the news. The Magdalene was left surrounded in the center of the circle, scanning the disciples gathered.

There were so many more than just the Twelve – she meant, the Eleven… that would take some getting used to, now that Judas had hanged himself. There was Cleophas and the friend that was his constant shadow – she reminded herself to get his name. Mary was nowhere to be seen, nor was John, but he assumed they were together. There were Phillip and Andrew and Simon-not-Peter. There were the Zebedees and the Alphaeuses and the Marcuses, of course – but where was Peter? They were especially supposed to tell Peter. She forged ahead: "I have seen Jesus!"

Immediately, the hubbub ceased, and everyone fell silent. Mary continued, "He just met me in the garden outside the tomb! I thought he was the gardener at first; but then He said my name, and I knew it was Him! He told me to come tell you..."

All eyes stared at her. Eventually, Thaddaeus ventured, "Now, Mary, we all wish that were so, but –"

"No, Thaddaeus, it's true. Remember, He told us He would be crucified and then raised to life after three days. Well? It's happened!" Mary's smile was bold and bright, but she still saw only faces of mourning and misery gathered around her. "Don't you believe me? Ladies, c'mon, help me out here!"

"Oh, it's true," Salome asserted. "The rest of us met two angels at the tomb – or was it three? Anyway – at least we assume they were angels; their clothes were bright white like lightning – and they asked us why we were looking for living people among the dead."

"Too soon, Salome, too soon." Zebedee pulled his wife close and tried to hush her with a hug.

"What do you mean, too soon? This is *not* a joke, you old wolf. Let me go!"

"Then one of them told us not to be afraid," blurted Susannah, "and I thought *yeah, right...*, but I didn't dare say anything."

John Mark snorted a laugh, producing a sharp elbow in his ribs from his mother. The men exchanged skeptical glances with one another: the younger ones clucked their tongues, but the older ones held theirs.

Joanna ignored them. "The second angel seemed to be the spokesman for the pair. He told us plainly that we were looking for Jesus, but He wasn't there because He had risen from the dead! Then he pointed to the empty table where the body had been placed."

THE EIGHT *FIRST* WORDS OF CHRIST

"I know it had been there because I *saw* Joseph and Nicodemus put Him there on Friday afternoon," Mary Alphaeus asserted, "The table was empty except for the grave clothes still lying there, also empty!" She looked back and forth between Clopas and James, willing them to believe her.

Mary Marcus, ever the hostess, tried to intervene. "Now, Mary, we're all just a bit overwrought from the events of the weekend. Why don't you ladies all come into the house, and I'll put on the water for some nice chamomile tea —"

"No!" Salome all but roared. "Zebedee, James, listen to me! We are not 'overwrought!'" Salome all but spat the word. "We saw Jesus with our own eyes not more than fifteen minutes ago! I held His left ankle in the dust! See! See, my sleeves are still dirty!"

Magdalene reinserted herself into the conversation — this was decidedly *not* the direction she had thought it would take. "He talked a lot about 'ascending.' He told me to tell you specifically that He is ascending to His Father and your Father, to His God and your God. I don't know how soon it's going to happen, but He was urgent."

Joanna leapt in as if her memory had suddenly poked her in the back. "But I don't think that's imminent, though, because the angels told us to be certain to tell you all that He is going ahead of us back to Galilee. They told us to tell you that you will see Him there. It sounded like He is planning to spend some time with us before He ascends to His Father." Joanna nodded submissively in Mary Magdalene's direction.

Magdalene gestured to the group as if to say, "Well?" Most of the men shuffled back and forth awkwardly, their thumbs in their belts, shifting their eyes among themselves when they weren't staring at the dirt of the courtyard. Mary Alphaeus and Salome looked to their husbands and sons for support, which was begrudgingly extracted, if at all. Joanna stood with hands on hips glaring at those who were having trouble accepting such glorious news, while Susanna clung to Mary Marcus and wanted nothing more than that cup of chamomile tea.

"Don't you believe us?" cried Mary. "Why? We are *five* witnesses of our Lord *alive*!"

"I tell you what, Mary," Matthew said, breaking the mostly male silence. "Thaddeus, Andrew, and I will go to the tomb and investigate."

"So the answer's no, you don't believe us!" Mary's eyes welled up with tears yet again that day, but this time, she refused to let them spill, angrily wiping them with the back of her sleeve. Matthew had wounded her to her core.

Joanna said what the rest of the women were thinking. "Fine! If three of you men go as "witnesses," maybe He'll greet you like He did us and maybe He won't, but you'll believe then, what? Because you're 'manly men.'" If Chuza heard of this outburst, she'd be in trouble, but she didn't care. This was so unfair!

"Wait! We're going with you!" Both Jameses kissed their mothers on their foreheads and moved to Matthew, Thaddeus, and Andrew by the door. "Then it will be five and five," James Alphaeus said.

"Or five *against* five," Joanna muttered, not quite under her breath, which was quickly turning to steam.

So while they should have been rejoicing and packing for a trip to Galilee, they all just sat and sulked while they waited the half-hour, forty-five minutes for the five

THE EIGHT *FIRST* WORDS OF CHRIST

to investigate the women's tale and return. Mary Marcus plied her guests with that chamomile tea until they were floating, but it didn't seem to relax the atmosphere much.

Finally, they heard a knock on the courtyard door; and John Mark ran to open it. Matthew led the entourage of men quietly back into the courtyard, and everyone gathered around, arms folded, anxious for the verdict. Zebedee's James had been elected spokesperson for the group.

"The ladies were right." A throaty gasp and a high-pitched squeal arose from the crowd, but James quieted them all with both hands. "That is to say, we found everything just as the women described. The tomb has been opened, and the grave clothes are lying on the stone table flat and empty." James let that much sink in before going on, "but there were no angels and, furthermore, no sign of Jesus."

"So, since we saw him and you didn't, you presume *us* to be crazy… or worse, lying! That's it! I'm going home!" Joanna had been smoldering for some time, and James just brought pitch and a flint. "I hope my husband has more sense than the rest of you louts!" With that Joanna swept out the door. The house of Herod would not rest any easier this night…

Mary Magdalene stepped forward regally. "I know what I saw, and I know what I heard. I may not have recognized Him immediately, but when He said my name, I *knew* it was Him. He is going to ascend to heaven, and I hope you don't all miss your opportunity to see Him before he does because of your lack of faith. Now, if you'll excuse me, Mary, I would like to go to my room."

"We will join you, Maggie," Salome said, grabbing Mary Alphaeus by the hand. "James and James, I am very disappointed in you, contradicting your own mothers this way; and Zebedee and Clopas, you can find your own suppers this evening. We will be dining with Mary." With that, the three women linked arms and strode into the house.

"I'm sorry, I need to use the facilities." Susanna burped softly and handed her cup to Mary Marcus. "Thank you for the tea. It was lovely," and she hurried into the house as well.

We will hear in the next Word Cleophas and his friend's perspective of this news from the women: "Moreover, some women of our company amazed us. They were at the tomb early in the morning, and when they did not find His body, they came back saying that they had even seen a vision of angels, who said that he was alive. Some of those who were with us went to the tomb and found it just as the women had said, but him they did not see." Moreover, we will hear Jesus' response to the disciples' unbelief in Word Four.

The second word Jesus had for us out the tomb was to "fear not." Don't be afraid. Don't live in fear. We will find this repeated in Words four and five as well as Jesus seeks to reassure His disciples with peace. Even in the midst of difficult and confusing circumstances, we must "let not our hearts be troubled nor be afraid." When one serves the mighty God of All Creation, can anything ultimately go wrong? "If God be for us, who can be against us." "With God, all things are possible." "Cast all your cares upon Him because He cares for you." In II Timothy 1:7, the Apostle Paul wrote, "for God gave us a spirit not of fear but of power and love and self-control." Fear may occasionally be healthy, but it is never one of God's intended gifts.

THE EIGHT *FIRST* WORDS OF CHRIST

Notice that with Christ's injunction not to fear came a mission with a message. The women were to "go" (we'll find this repeated in Word Seven), this time to Jesus' "brothers," and to tell them, too, to "go" to Galilee, where they will eventually see Him. It is interesting that Jesus called the disciples his "brothers." (We know He meant not His physical half-brothers here but rather His disciples, for that is to whom the women went.) We are reminded of the moment in Matt. 12:46-50 when Mary and Jesus' half-brothers came to Him and wanted to speak to Him while He was ministering because they thought He may have lost His mind; and He pointed to His disciples and said, "Here are my mother and my brothers! For whoever does the will of my Father in heaven is my brother and sister and mother." These people had first been followers, then servants, then students and disciples. In the upper room, a little before His death, He called them His friends. Now here, after His resurrection, He calls them His brothers. These same men, however, had most recently denied, forsaken, and run from Him – one even left his bed clothes in a soldier's hand and fled naked into the night! Still, He called them His brothers. The *Jamieson-Fausset-Brown Bible Commentary* quotes one Bishop Hall as having said, in effect, that our sins simply can't "unbrother" us from Christ.[2]

---

2 https://biblehub.com/commentaries/john/20-17.htm Jamieson-Fausset-Brown

For Further Contemplation and Discussion:

Of what were the women so afraid that it kept them from immediately delivering such good news to the disciples? (Think especially of Susanna's thinking above.)

Why do you think Jesus essentially repeated the same message to the women that the angels had already given them at the tomb?

THE EIGHT *FIRST* WORDS OF CHRIST

Other than the fact that no one had ever risen singlehandedly from their own death before, why else might the disciples not have believed the women, except for the fact that they were women?

Why is it important not to be afraid when one is given a job to do? How effective is a fearful person in accomplishing a task or mission? Why or why not?

CHAPTER FIVE

Word Three
"O foolish men, and slow of heart to believe in all that the prophets have spoken!"

LET ME PAUSE for a quick discussion concerning the ordering of these Words. Unlike on the cross, where we had a static location and were subject to all the natural laws of God's Creation, all bets are off with Jesus' resurrection. Here, we will find Him in a body (*and clothes!*) that can pass through walls and locked doors, a body that can transmogrify and take on a different form so as to make Him unrecognizable to even His closest disciples, a body that moves outside of the constraints of time and space. In such a world, it is quite easily imaginable that Jesus might have been two places at one-time, making a certain and clear chronology precarious at best. Still, it was Earth in Time and Space so I've leaned away from putting Him in two places at once for the purpose of this book, suggesting it only as a remote possibility in the final Word.

THE EIGHT *FIRST* WORDS OF CHRIST

That said, presumably, Jesus's appearance to Peter (as all but passingly mentioned in Luke 24:34 and corroborated by Paul in I Cor. 15:5) must have taken place in late morning or early afternoon on Sunday. This makes complete sense when we know Jesus and His heart. Both Luke and John tell us that Peter left the empty tomb, having seen the empty grave clothes and the face cloth or bandana folded and laid neatly aside, "wondering," not "believing" as John the Beloved had. Luke tells us he merely went away, but John tells us he went home, not to Capernaum but to where he was staying in Jerusalem, possibly the home of Mary Marcus and her son John Mark, possibly another location. Knowing Jesus, He would not allow His right-hand man and key apostle to wonder too long, especially knowing that Peter had denied Him as He'd predicted he would and had wept bitter tears because of it. It would make sense for Peter to be the third person to whom He would appear after His resurrection.

Nothing, however, is recorded of what Jesus *said* in this particular exchange so we cannot count its words here in this study; but it is interesting to me, as we will see when we study Word Six, that there is no mention made then of Peter's denial. We will discuss there about Jesus addressing Peter three times with essentially the same message and how that may or may not relate to Peter's having denied Christ thrice during His trial, but suffice it to say here that I believe it was in this earlier meeting that Peter confessed His denial of Christ, received His forgiveness and grace, and was restored to His place of service in God's Kingdom. Perhaps no words are recorded because perhaps no words were needed.

Jesus' third Word takes place on the road to and in the town of Emmaus, a small village sixty stadia or about seven miles east-northeast of Jerusalem. After His meeting with Peter, we find Jesus meeting with two of His other followers on the Road to Emmaus: Cleophas (also spelled Cleopas, the male form of Cleopatra) and an unnamed disciple. Linguistically, we should assume that Cleopas and Clopas (two different spellings in the Greek) Alphaeus, husband of Mary and father of James, also known as James the Lesser and one of the Twelve Apostles, are two different people although Catholic and Eastern Orthodox traditions believe them to be the same and that Clopas is a brother of Jesus' stepfather, Joseph. The belief that Clopas and Joseph were brothers stems from the historian Hegesippus, writing in A.D. 180 of having interviewed the Apostle Jude's, Jesus' younger half-brother's, grandsons years earlier, who had reported that Clopas was Joseph's brother, making his sons Jesus' cousins. This was recorded by the historian Eusebius.[3]

Knowing (with admitted uncertainty) a little about Cleopas, we now wonder as to the identity of the unnamed disciple. You may remember that, in addition to sending the Twelve out on mission in Luke 9, Jesus later gathered seventy (or seventy-two) men to send out on a second mission in Luke 10. While the identity of these men are not listed in Scripture, an ancient Greek text entitled *On the Seventy Apostles of Christ* and originally attributed to the historian Hippolytus of Rome, lists Cleopas as the second name of the Seventy and eventually "bishop of Jerusalem."[4] If (and this is a huge stretch) we were

---

3 Eusebius of Caesarea, Church History, Book III, ch. 11.
4 Roberts, Alexander; Donaldson, James; Coxe, A. Cleveland, eds. (1886). "Appendix to the Works of Hippolytus; containing Dubious and Spurious Pieces". The Ante-Nicene Fathers: Translations of the Writings of the Fathers Down to A. D. 325. Vol.

to believe this list ordered by the pairs by which Jesus sent the Seventy out, we would have to place Cleopas with the first name on the list, who is James, Jesus' half-brother and also an eventual bishop of Jerusalem. While this might make sense for them to have been paired with one another from the beginning of their public ministry with Jesus, there is no evidence to suggest that James began to follow Jesus until His appearance to him after the resurrection (and yet to come in this chronology). Matthias is the name that follows Cleopas in *On the Seventy Apostles of Christ*; however, it is unlikely Dr. Luke would not name him here since he later names him as the disciple God chooses to replace Judas Iscariot in the Twelve. I guess we'll have to wait until heaven to find out who he was, assuming it wasn't Cleopas' wife! For now, we'll just call him "Friend."

"Jesus Himself drew near and went with them." There is no indication that Jesus, whom we had last seen in the environs of the tomb outside Jerusalem, had been following the two disciples; and if my hypothesis of His meeting with Peter is true, it is unlikely He had gone ahead of them and was waiting for them to pass Him on the road. To me, there is a sense of His merely "appearing" on the road with them, a sudden emergence into their conscious awareness and then his falling in to walk with them along the way, as if once two and now three.

We do not know *how* God kept them from recognizing Him as Jesus, although their active lack of faith and expectation surely played a part in it: one does not normally see or hear what one does not suppose is possible to be seen

---

V. translated by J. H. McMahon (American reprint of the Edinburgh ed.). Buffalo: Christian Literature Company. pp. –256.

or heard. Mark says in 16:12, "He appeared in a different *form*" (emphasis added). Obviously, despite being only inches away, they didn't recognize His face, His clothes, His gait, or His voice, the latter being the most interesting to disguise; but the actor in me wonders how far from the truth was His disguise. Did He appear much older or much younger than his thirty-three years? Did He appear to be far wealthier than He had ever been in life? Had He any disfigurement; or more likely, was He now strikingly handsome when before "he had no form or majesty that we should look at him, and no beauty that we should desire him (Isaiah 53:2)." God adds "Greatest Makeup Artist in All History" to His portfolio!

Jesus shows Himself to be a sterling conversationalist here with a question as His opening gambit: "So… what are you talking about so animatedly as we walk along?" He doesn't waste any time but gets right to the heart of their conversation, inserting Himself affably and effortlessly. When they defer an immediate answer by questioning how this "visitor" could possibly *not* have heard about Jesus' crucifixion, it gives us insight into exactly how big a deal this particular crucifixion had been to the populace as a whole, not just to His disciples. At least the disciples saw it as such. Jesus merely asks, "What things?", again, a question designed to get them to talk.

And talk they did. What follows are six verses of diatribe as Cleopas and Friend unpack a nutshell of the Gospel: who Jesus was and what He did; what the Sanhedrin and Rome did to Him in the end; what hopes and dreams the disciples had placed in Him; the report of the women on this, the third day; and the report of the men who had followed up on the women's report. The discussion topic

THE EIGHT *FIRST* WORDS OF CHRIST

before them would certainly carry them the rest of the way to Emmaus.

It was obvious to Jesus anyway, if not to Cleopas and Friend, that they and the other disciples had not believed the women's report; and He responded to that transgression appropriately with Word 3: "O foolish men, and slow of heart to believe in all that the prophets have spoken!" I'm sure Cleopas and Friend were a bit taken aback by this reproof from "a total stranger"; but as always, I'm sure Jesus spoke it with such authority that they couldn't help but listen and accept the chastisement. He was about to back it up with some pretty thorough teaching as well.

Jesus went on: "'Was it not necessary that the Christ should suffer these things and enter into his glory?' And beginning with Moses and all the Prophets, he interpreted to them in all the Scriptures the things concerning himself." Jesus had more than an afternoon's worth of material from which to draw for this teaching. The Old Testament Prophets had very blatantly portrayed the Anointed One as having to suffer before being glorified. No less than Isaiah, chief of the Major Prophets, spends all of what we know as chapter 53 portraying the Suffering Servant.[5] Some scholars suggest there are as many as 300 Old Testament prophetic scriptures that Jesus' life fulfilled! In her article "Old Testament Prophesies of Jesus," Mary Fairchild quotes Peter Stoner and Robert Newman in their book *Science Speaks* on the statistical

---

[5] https://www.gotquestions.org/suffering-servant-Isaiah-53.html . Accessed June 13, 2024. See this passage for an excellent treatise on ancient rabbinical references to this as a Messianic prophesy. Contemporary rabbis dismiss Isaiah 53, and it alone of all the Old Testament is never read in contemporary Jewish services.

improbability of one man fulfilling, accidentally or deliberately, even *eight* of the prophecies Jesus fulfilled. "The chance of this happening, they say, is 1 in 10^{17} power. Stoner presents a scenario that illustrates the magnitude of such odds:

"Suppose that we take 10^{17} silver dollars and lay them on the face of Texas. They will cover all of the state two feet deep. Now mark one of these silver dollars and stir the whole mass thoroughly, all over the state. Blindfold a man and tell him that he can travel as far as he wishes, but he must pick up one silver dollar and say that this is the right one. What chance would he have of getting the right one? Just the same chance that the prophets would have had of writing these eight prophecies and having them all come true in any one man, from their day to the present time, providing they wrote using their own wisdom."[6]

Just a few of the prophesies mentioned by "Moses and the Prophets" of which Jesus may have reminded them that day might have included:

- Messiah would be born of a woman (Genesis 3:15)
- Messiah would be in Abraham's line (Genesis 12:3, 22:18)
- Messiah would be in Isaac's line (Genesis 17:19, 21:12)
- Messiah would be in Jacob's line (Numbers 24:17)
- Messiah would come from Judah's tribe (Genesis 49:10)

---

[6] Fairchild, Mary. "Old Testament Prophecies of Jesus." Learn Religions, Sep. 3, 2021, learnreligions.com/prophecies-of-jesus-fulfilled-700159.

THE EIGHT *FIRST* WORDS OF CHRIST

- Messiah would be heir to David's throne (II Samuel 7:12-13, Isaiah 9:7)
- Messiah's way would be prepared (Isaiah 40:3-5)
- A forerunner would precede Messiah (Malachi 3:1)
- Messiah's own people would reject Him (Psalm 69:8, Isaiah 53:3)
- Messiah would bring light to Galilee (Isaiah 9:1-2)
- Messiah would enter Jerusalem on a donkey (Zechariah 11:12)
- Messiah would be betrayed (Psalm 41:9, Zech. 11:12-13)
- Messiah's hands and feet would be pierced (Psalm 22:16, Zechariah 12:10)
- Soldiers would gamble for His clothes (Psalm 22:18)
- Messiah would be buried with the rich (Isaiah 53:9)
- Messiah would rise from the dead (Psalm 16:10, 49:15)

Imagine walking along and having an intensive Bible Study with Jesus covering just the Scriptures and topics above. I imagine it would be eye-opening and mind-blowing for any of us, but certainly it would have been so for Cleopas and Friend as they experienced these events firsthand and tried to make sense of them in the moment.

I'm sure they were so absorbed in conversation they barely noticed entering the environs of Emmaus, but Jesus did, and "He acted as if He were going farther." If it were ever needed, therein lies the justification for every Christian theatrician who ever lived: Jesus "acted." Jesus made a pretense of having to be somewhere else, of having an agenda other than the one He had, which was to finish His conversation with these two beloved disciples and reveal Himself to them as very much alive and risen from the dead.

And Jesus was a *good* and very convincing actor, to the point that Cleopas and Friend *implored* Him not to leave but rather to come in and spend the night with them. Perhaps they hoped to hear more evidence from Scripture of how their Rabbi Jesus had fulfilled other Old Testament prophecies. Perhaps they wanted simply to know more about their mysterious traveling companion, not realizing that both desires were really one and the same. Whatever the reason for their wanting Him near, He chose to stay and to reveal Himself to them.

The delight of this revelation is that it came about over the most ordinary of circumstances: an evening meal. "When he was at table with them, he took the bread and blessed and broke it and gave it to them." Immediately, we are reminded of what we call The Last Supper or Jesus feeding the 5,000 or the 4,000. Assuming that Cleopas and Friend were at least a part of the Seventy, we might assume they had at least witnessed the miraculous feedings and possibly any number of daily meals with Jesus. We do well to remember that it is often in the common, most ordinary moments of life that we see Jesus and recognize Him as He truly is. "Then their eyes were opened and they recognized Him…"

"…And He vanished from their sight." Poof! (Don't you wish the Bible had sound effects?) That was it. The very moment they recognized Him for Who He really was, He was gone. How must Cleopas and Friend have *felt* in that moment? Surprised? Of course. Disappointed? Maybe, but I think joy was more overwhelming. "It's Him! It's

THE EIGHT *FIRST* WORDS OF CHRIST

Jesus! Mary and the ladies were right after all! He is alive, and (the very next thought) He's appeared to *us*! Of all people!" (I don't imagine for an instant that it was *only* the Twelve who had argued over who was greatest in the Kingdom of God.) "He was here! He spent all afternoon teaching us. Wow! *Did not our hearts burn within us while he talked to us on the road, while he opened to us the Scriptures?"*

Hearts now burning with the urgency to reunite with the other disciples and all thoughts of food banished, they immediately got up and hurried the seven miles back to Jerusalem. At a slightly above average pace, albeit the end of the day, this would have taken them almost two hours and would have put them back in Jerusalem in the early to mid-evening, 7:30-8:30ish. They went where the disciples were all staying, which I have established for the purpose of this study as the home of Mary Marcus; and found all Eleven apostles there along with others; but what they had hoped to bring as news or at least as a corroboration of the women's proclamation earlier in the day was relegated to fourth place. Simon Peter was there and had already reported to all those gathered Jesus' private appearance to him earlier in the day. Not to be outdone or dissuaded, Cleopas and Friend told them what had happened to them on the way to Emmaus, and how they recognized Jesus when He broke the bread.

Mark, who was quite possibly present for the events, gives us a bit different ending to this part of the story than Dr. Luke, who, by his own admission, was reliant on research from first-hand sources. I should perhaps admit a slight prejudice in favor of Mark's account. First, I believe that Mark the Evangelist, author of the gospel and associate of Peter, and John Mark, cousin of Barnabas and future associate of Paul, are indeed the same person. I believe that he was of mixed parentage, having a Jewish mother named Mary and a Roman father, possible last name Marcus, who were well placed in Jerusalem society. I believe that John Mark first appears in Scripture as the rich, young ruler in the Synoptics: Mark 10:17-27, Matthew 19:16-22, and Luke 18:18-30 (so I believe that man *did* go and sell all he had and returned to follow Jesus). I believe that, just as John the beloved never mentions his own name or the names of his family members in His gospel so also did Mark not mention himself or his family members by name in his gospel; therefore, I also believe, along with a growing number of scholars, that the man who fled naked from the Garden of Gethsemane at the time of Jesus' arrest was also John Mark, as Mark's gospel is the only one to include this account. All of this, however, is conversation for another day.

I bring it up here only in support of my attempt to reconcile both Mark's and Luke's accounts of the end of Cleopas and Friend's story. Mark gives their story short shrift in just two verses (Mark 16:12-13), where he states in v. 13, "And they went back and told the rest, but they did not believe them." What ironic and just comeuppance for two who had earlier so easily dismissed the testimony of the women! Luke's account, however, has Peter beating Cleopas and Friend to the punch. He has already reported Jesus' meeting with Him to the other disciples gathered in Mary's home, and they apparently believed Peter. How could Cleopas and Friend then tell their story and not be believed?

It is possible that Dr. Luke, in his otherwise meticulous research, got the order of events slightly muddled.

THE EIGHT *FIRST* WORDS OF CHRIST

It is possible (and even perhaps likely) that Peter was so exhausted by his meeting with the Lord and the great relief he experienced afterward that he did not somehow make it back to the rest of the group until after Cleopas and Friend returned. They had reported their experience of their afternoon with Jesus to the gathered disciples, who didn't believe them, only to have Peter come crashing into the mourning party and testify to his meeting with Jesus, at which point they all believed. Then Cleopas and Friend related their story all over again for Peter's sake. While they were in the middle of this *second* account of their afternoon, "while they were still talking" (Luke 24:36), Jesus showed up to deliver Word 4.

For Further Contemplation and Discussion:

If the tale were told of you and your "bestie" traveling on a road and meeting Jesus, and one of you were named and one unnamed, which would you be and why?

Does the spectacle and theatricality of this account (Jesus' disguise, Jesus the actor, the timing of their return to the other disciples) intrigue you? Why?

THE EIGHT *FIRST* WORDS OF CHRIST

Of all 300 passages from the Old Testament that Jesus fulfilled and will yet fulfill, which ones would you wish He would explain to you if you were to have opportunity to ask Him about them. (Oh, and by the way, you *do* have opportunity to do so, you know…)

How do you approach the Bible when it occasionally *appears* to contradict itself from one passage to another? Do you immediately think *it* must be wrong or *we* must be wrong? How do you reconcile differences in the Scripture?

CHAPTER SIX

Word Four

"Peace be unto you." Part I:
"Receive Holy Spirit…I am sending the promise of My Father upon you."

LUKE TELLS US THAT, while Cleophas and Friend were still talking, Jesus showed up; but we learn a few more details from John the Beloved in 20:19. We learn that it was "evening," still of that first day of the week. Here we must observe that John continues to use Roman rather than Jewish reckoning of time as he has throughout the crucifixion and resurrection section of his gospel. In the same way we would reckon the time today, this appearance of Jesus took place on Sunday in the evening (what would have been the *beginning* of Jewish Monday). John also tells us that the disciples were together, "the doors being locked where the disciples were for fear of the Jews," *i.e.* the Sanhedrin, the Jewish leaders. It was in that circumstance that "Jesus came and stood among them and said to them, 'Peace be with you.'" Jesus didn't "melt" through the wall or door and linger there. No! Just as He had vanished right before Cleopas and Friend's eyes the moment they recognized Him, so now did He reappear – poof! – standing right in their midst!

Now I must admit to you that I am no Greek scholar, nor have I ever taken a class in the Greek language: I know just enough Greek to be dangerous, but I do know how to look things up. When I first read 'Peace be with you," I assumed the Greek word used was *shalom,* since I knew that word, and I knew it means *peace.* If I were publishing a book, however, I needed to be certain of such things (because my readers are way smarter than I am) so I looked this up in an interlinear Bible (which has the English translation following along with both the Greek and the English transposition of Greek), and I found out that this was not the more generic word *shalom* but rather the more specific word *eirene,* indicating peace of mind or quietness of spirit. Jesus Himself, a Man Whom many in the room still thought to be dead, just appeared and stood among them in the middle of a room where the doors were locked! Jesus' first words to His disciples were more akin to "Don't scream! Settle down. Hush... Quietness and rest be yours."

Luke picks up the story at this point (24:37-43), "But they were startled and frightened and thought they saw a spirit. And He said to them, 'Why are you troubled, and why do doubts arise in your hearts? See my hands and my feet, that it is I myself. Touch me and see. For a spirit does not have flesh and bones as you see that I have.' And when He had said this, He showed them His hands and His feet. And while they still disbelieved for joy and were marveling, He said to them, 'Have you anything here to eat?' They gave Him a piece of broiled fish and possibly some honeycomb, and He took it and ate before them."

I find it so interesting that the women had needed no such rebuke when Jesus appeared to them earlier in the day. They apparently had the opposite problem. So firmly did both Mary Magdalene and the other women immediately and resolutely believe that Jesus Himself stood before them that they immediately fell at his feet, grabbed Him, and worshiped Him! When He appeared to all of them, however, in an even more miraculous way, appearing in the middle of a room that everyone knew to be locked and barred against the Jews, He chastised them for doubting.

Jesus had no intention of leaving them in their doubt, however. He proceeded to show them the nail prints in His hands and feet. John includes showing them His side because he alone mentions the piercing of Jesus' side in his Gospel. Luke says He even invites them to touch Him to see that He is really Jesus in "the flesh and bones" although there is no record of anyone taking Him up on the offer. Again, it is interesting that the women had been unafraid to hold onto Jesus, but the men might even have been hesitant to touch Him.

In verse 41, Luke describes a subtle but definite shift in the reason behind their doubts. As they observed (and perhaps touched) the scars that could only have come from Jesus' wounds on the cross, they stopped doubting out of unbelief and fear and started doubting instead that anything so wonderful could truly be happening to them! They moved from the doubt of Zechariah when Gabriel announced that John would be born to him and Elizabeth in their old age to the doubt of Mary, who was

THE EIGHT *FIRST* WORDS OF CHRIST

simply overjoyed to be selected as the Messiah's mother but wondered how such a glorious thing might come about. While Jesus rebukes, chastises, and condemns the first kind of doubt and unbelief, I believe He somewhat enjoys, encourages, and condones the second. Here He asked for something to eat, and they immediately supplied Him with a leftover piece of broiled fish (in *all* the original manuscripts) and possibly with a hunk of honeycomb as well (as included in some of the original manuscripts). I believe Jesus enjoyed watching the disciples stare at him as He ate this simple snack and licked His fingers and smacked His lips profusely afterward, *especially* if the honeycomb were included!

Returning to John's account, the disciples believed and were overjoyed to see Jesus! Again, Jesus had to calm them down with another, "*Eirene hymin*: Quietness and rest be yours." Again, as he did back in Luke 9 and 10, He commissions them all as apostles, as "sent ones": "As the Father has sent me, even so I am sending you." Then, He did what He came to do that evening: He breathed on them and said, "*Labete Pneuma Hagion*; Receive Holy Spirit."

The Greek word for "breathed" here is used nowhere else in the New Testament; but interestingly, it is used one other place in the Septuagint, the Greek Translation of the Old Testament; and that is in Genesis 2:7: "then the Lord God formed the man of dust from the ground and *breathed* into his nostrils the breath of life, and the man became a living creature." During Ezekiel's vision of the valley of dry bones in 37:9, God told Ezekiel to "Prophesy to the breath; prophesy, son of man, and say to the breath, 'Thus says the Lord God: come from the four winds, O breath, and breathe on these slain, that they may live.'"

After Jesus had told Nicodemus in John 3 about the necessity of being born again, in v. 8, He explained the role that the *Pneuma,* the Spirit, the Breath plays in the process of being born again: "The wind blows where it wishes, and you hear its sound, but you do not know where it comes from or where it goes. So it is with everyone who is born of the Spirit." We need to remember, too, that more than just ten of the Twelve are in this room: Cleopas and Friend are there, as possibly are some of the women and other unmentioned disciples. Jesus here is breathing new life into *all* His followers.

Scholars have made much of the absence of an article or adjective in the phrase, "Receive Holy Spirit": it is not *the* Holy Spirit or *a* Holy Spirit or *My* Holy Spirit or countless other descriptors – simply "Receive Holy Spirit." Much has also been theorized to justify Jesus imparting the Holy Spirit at all prior to His return to heaven. John wrote in 7:39, "Now this [promise of living waters flowing from believers' hearts] He said about the Spirit, Whom those who believed in Him were to receive, for as yet the Spirit had not been given, *because Jesus was not yet glorified.*" After His resurrection, however, Jesus *is* in His glorified body at least, if not in His glorified estate yet in heaven; and He is God, after all, so I would venture to say He can do as He pleases. Still, however, just the night before His crucifixion, Jesus had told His disciples, referring to the Holy Spirit, "Nevertheless, I tell you the truth: it is to your advantage that I go away, for *if I do not go away, the Helper will not come to you. But if I go, I will send him to you.*" Jesus had not yet "gone" so this must not be the "sending" or impartation to which Jesus had referred in the upper room.

THE EIGHT *FIRST* WORDS OF CHRIST

It is interesting that Jesus uses the same verb, *labete*, here concerning the Spirit as He did at their meal on Thursday when He established communion with the bread and the cup: in Matthew and Mark, He told them to *labete* the bread; and in Luke, He told them to *labete* the cup. There, the word is often translated as "take." This interchangeability of the English "take" and "receive" is interesting. Both words imply a choice, and we use them in some customary ways. For example, we speak of a man "taking" a bride, and traditional marriage vows ask if we "take" one another as husband and wife; but would it be any different if we spoke of "receiving" one another? We often use the words interchangeably when talking of salvation: did you "take" Jesus as your Savior, or did You "receive" Jesus as your savior? Most likely, a believer would answer affirmatively to either question. Why would it be any different to say, "I received Jesus" than it would be to say, "I received God" or "I received Holy Spirit"? In our text, Jesus tells His disciples to "receive" or to "take" Holy Spirit. Once the disciples did so, a possession, an ownership of a particular kind was their new reality.

This impartation of the Holy Spirit to the disciples was perhaps not markedly different from the impartation He gave both to the Twelve and to the Seventy when He sent them out earlier: the word *apostle* means "one who is sent." You may remember He gave them *power* over demons and disease, and we know that this power comes from the Holy Spirit when it is manifest on earth; but this time, the impartation came with the imperative to "receive Holy Spirit." In this new reality of a Jesus who came and went in mysterious and inexplicable ways, it was as if Jesus were saying, "Depend on Him as you have depended on me." Jesus provided an "interim" presence, if you will, of the Holy Spirit to His followers to be with them prior to Pentecost. As we have subsequently learned, when Jesus will later say in Word Seven, "Behold, I am with you always, even to the end of the age," He meant in the Person of the Holy Spirit.

It is interesting to note that Jesus did *not* spend the forty days between His resurrection and ascension focused on explaining his crucifixion, burial, and resurrection – He left that for the Holy Spirit to instruct the apostles later and us now. His Words in His appearances seemed rather to be focused for the most part on moving forward the story of the Kingdom, on the mission and the future. This brings us to John 20:23, perhaps the most potentially troublesome and misunderstood part of Word Four theologically: "If you forgive the sins of any, they are forgiven them; if you withhold forgiveness from any, it is withheld." As I approach this discussion, I feel more trepidation than Jesus must have felt when He chose first to say to the paralytic who was let down through the roof by his friends, "Your sins are forgiven" instead of "Rise, take up your bed and walk." Pharisees still walk among us, but may Holy Spirit help me rightly divide the Word of Truth!

This particular impartation of the Holy Spirit apparently came with discernment concerning the forgiveness and retention of sins. I hasten to add that this discernment has continued as part of the Holy Spirit's ministry: as Jesus Himself said, "And when He [Holy Spirit] comes, He will convict the world concerning sin and righteousness and judgment: concerning sin, because they do not believe in me" (John 16:8-9). Nineteenth century Bible scholar and theologian Charles John Ellicott

THE EIGHT *FIRST* WORDS OF CHRIST

writes in his *Bible Commentary for English Readers,* "God has promised forgiveness wherever there is repentance; He has not promised repentance wherever there is sin."[7] He goes on to make some important points about the English verb tenses which will help in our understanding. To paraphrase his text for the contemporary reader: "If you agree with God that He has forgiven someone's sins, their sinful condition has changed and they are forgiven them; if you withhold forgiveness from any, agreeing with God that their condition remains unchanged for lack of repentance or confession or whatever reason, it is withheld." Jesus was not here giving the power to forgive or condemn sins: the Pharisees were correct when they said that only God has the power to forgive sins because it is Him against whom we have trespassed; He is the Creditor to Whom we are forever indebted, one way or the other. Additionally, if God did not send His own Son Jesus into the world to condemn the world (John 3:17), I very much doubt He sent Peter or John or me or you to condemn it either.

To put it another way, English theologian and minister Joseph Benson in his multi-volume *Commentary on the New and Old Testaments* suggests we have (1) power to interpret scripture, action, word, and emotion to speak authoritatively concerning pardon, *i.e.* "declaring with authority the Christian terms of pardon," (2) the power to inflict and remit church discipline as needed, and even (3) " the gift of discerning the spirits of men in such perfection, as to be able to declare with certainty to particular persons in question whether or not they were in a state of pardon and acceptance with God."[8] In a nutshell,

---

7 https://biblehub.com/commentaries/john/20-23.htm
8 https://biblehub.com/commentaries/john/20-21.htm

then, the forgiveness and retention of sin are the Creditor's alone to address with each debtor. Our responsibility as His ambassadors is simply to assure the repentant debtors of their forgiveness and to note to ourselves those who remain unrepentant.

Finally, back to Luke's account, "Then he said to them, 'These are My words that I spoke to you while I was still with you, that everything written about Me in the Law of Moses and the Prophets and the Psalms must be fulfilled.' Then he opened their minds to understand the Scriptures, and said to them, 'Thus it is written, that the Christ should suffer and on the third day rise from the dead, and that repentance for the forgiveness of sins should be proclaimed in His name to all nations, beginning from Jerusalem. You are witnesses of these things. And behold, I am sending the promise of My Father upon you; but stay in the city until you are clothed with power from on high.'" Jesus ends the evening with clarification and assurance that there is yet to come another outpouring of His Holy Spirit upon them, and that they are to wait there in Jerusalem for that to happen.

The evening's meeting ends there, but Jesus' first day out of the grave had been eventful indeed! The narrative ends, and we are left to wonder whether Jesus left this particular meeting by vanishing or by using the door; for John the Beloved immediately points out that one of the Twelve, Thomas (his Hebrew name) Didymus (his Hellenistic name, both of which mean *twin*), was not in attendance when Jesus appeared that night so the other disciples sought him out and testified, "We have seen the Lord!" Let's see: it had only taken the testimonies of five women; Peter; Cleopas and Friend; Jesus' appearance Himself to them; His rebuke of their unbelief; and the sight (and possibly touch) of His hands, feet, and side; but hey, yep, yep, yep – their faith was now certain!

We could speculate endlessly concerning where Thomas had been (he was apparently not hard for the disciples to find) and why he was not with the others; but true to his Eyore-like character, I'm certain he was in deep mourning, still grieving the loss of his Master; and unlike his brothers, who had locked themselves away for fear of the Jews, Thomas seems to be out and about, almost daring them to come get him. After all, he was the disciple who had said, when Jesus, despite his followers' protests, said He was going to return to Bethany to take care of their sick friend Lazarus, "Let us also go, that we may die with Him" (John 11:16). John so beautifully foreshadows Word 5 when Thomas replies to the news of His risen Lord, "Unless I see in his hands the mark of the nails and place my finger into the mark of the nails, and place my hand into his side, I will never believe." Another beloved disciple is going to need a little… convincing.

For Further Contemplation and Discussion:

In what circumstances do you find yourself in need of more than simple *shalom;* when do you need Jesus to bring *eirene* to you, when your world is in a kerfuffle and you're ready to scream?

Why do you think the male disciples seemed to have so much more trouble believing in and accepting the resurrection than the women. Think Biblically rather than culturally.

THE EIGHT *FIRST* WORDS OF CHRIST

In these days of Zoom meetings and FaceTimes, there is much to be said for being in the same room with other humans. Would you consider "breathing" on someone who is experiencing either doubt and fear or a commissioning to ministry, trusting the Holy Spirit to meet them in new ways?

How might this chapter have changed your understanding of forgiving and withholding forgiveness from others?

CHAPTER SEVEN

Word Five

"Peace be unto you" Part II: "Blessed are those who have not seen and yet have believed."

Eight days later...

The Greek is very specific. Eight days. Eight days from a Sunday. To my mind, that cannot be the "next day" Monday but "Monday week" as they say in the South. *After* eight days. In my research, however, I was genuinely amazed that most scholars without question say this next Word took place on the following *Sunday*. They suggest that the first Sunday be included in the count as part of the eight days. Many of them go to great lengths to say that the disciples decided, from the very beginning, to make Sunday meetings a regular commemoration of the Lord's resurrection and that Jesus somehow solemnized that decision by showing up the following Sunday, too. I wouldn't choose it as a hill on which to die, but it's now the following *Monday* in my book – quite literally.

THE EIGHT *FIRST* WORDS OF CHRIST

What is more interesting to me than the day of the week upon which it takes place is the question of where Jesus *existed* when He wasn't appearing to His disciples. This Man Who has spent the last three years in public ministry dependent upon others to care for His needs, Who famously said to one who would follow Him, "The foxes have holes and the birds of the air have nests, but the Son of Man has nowhere to lay His head," and Who was known for His penchant for spending time alone in solitary places – did He now seek refuge in some heretofore unknown solitary place, visit tribes or nations He could not have visited while in His human body, or did He exist on some other earthly plane? He had proven He *could* eat, but did He *need* to eat? Did He need to sleep? What *needs*, if any, will our glorified bodies have?

But enough musing. Eight days later, every indication suggests that the disciples were all together again in the same place they had been eight days earlier; but this time, Thomas was with them. The doors were still locked, presumably out of the disciples' continuing, collective fear of the Jewish leaders, when suddenly, as before, "Jesus came and stood among them and said, '*Eirene hymin*; Peace be with you.'" It hasn't happened often enough to be a ritual yet, but so far, all is the same. This time, however, Jesus immediately turns to Thomas and says, "Put your finger here and see my hands; and put out your hand and place it in my side. Do not disbelieve but believe." What a Twilight Zone moment for Thomas! Not only does Jesus immediately show Thomas and the other disciples that He knew exactly what their previous conversation had been, but He also demonstrates Thomas as His foremost reason for and purpose in this appearance that evening. The Shepherd is ever after the one lost sheep.

It is interesting that there is no indication, for all the adamance of his first proclamation, that Thomas ever did actually put His fingers in the nail prints and stick his hand into Jesus' pierced side although I think we're fairly safe to imagine him falling to his knees when he answered Him, "My Lord and my God!" The adamant doubter who had essentially said, "I will no way, by no other means *ever* believe!" was now proclaiming Jesus' deity! While Peter had been privileged first to identify Jesus as the Anointed One and the *Son* of the Living God (Matt. 16:16), Thomas was the first to acknowledge Jesus as God *Himself*. If one doesn't believe in the resurrection of Jesus, one doesn't believe in Him at all.

Jesus took Thomas' response at "faith value," as a true statement of His belief in Him as Master and God of his life. The *Pulpit Commentary* puts it this way: "but it [the privilege of declaring God's deity] was reserved for the most depressed and skeptical mind of them all, the honest doubter, the man who needed immediate and irresistible evidence, infallible proofs, triumphant, invincible demonstrations – it was reserved for Thomas to say TO HIM, and to say unrebuked, uncondemned, by the risen Lord, 'MY LORD AND MY GOD!' ... This was the birth cry of Christendom!... Thomas doubted [so] that the Church might believe" [emphasis in original].[9] This birth cry is the climax of John's Gospel!

Jesus said to him, "Have you believed because you have seen me?" Notice that Jesus didn't say, "Have you believed because you touched me?" Again, there is no indication that Thomas ever followed through on his desire to touch Jesus' scars. "Blessed are those who have not seen and yet have believed." Note by definition this is a stray

---

9 https://biblehub.com/commentaries/john/20-28.htm

benediction, but it is the essence of Word Five. Thomas was happy and favored to have seen the resurrected Christ face to face, but *happier and more favored* will be those who believe *without* having seen. That is the very definition of faith according to Hebrews 11:1: "Now faith is the assurance of things hoped for, the conviction of things *not seen*" [emphasis added]. The less our faith needs sensory evidence, the stronger it is. The *Geneva Study Bible* says, "True faith depends upon the mouth of God and not upon the eyes of the flesh."[10]

Again, we do not know if this was the conclusion of the meeting. It seems altogether a very brief encounter: one almost wonders why Jesus didn't appear privately to Thomas as He did Peter except that Thomas's declaration had been public, to His fellow disciples, so it was important that they witness his revelation and faith. Again, I prefer to think Jesus didn't merely "chastise and run" but rather continued to spend a little more time with those He loved so well. After all, it is here that John goes on to say, "Now Jesus did many other signs in the presence of the disciples, which are not written in this book." Like any author, John had to be selective in what He included and left out of his book. John goes on to give us his filter, his purpose for including the events and incidences he did in his book: "…but these are written so that you may believe that Jesus is the Christ, the Son of God, and that by believing you may have life in his name." John's Gospel has come full circle from John 1:12-13: "But to all who did receive him, who believed in his name, he gave the right to become children of God, who were born, not of blood nor of the will of the flesh nor of the will of man,

---

[10] https://biblehub.com/commentaries/john/20-29.htm

but of God." John's desire is the same as Christ's desire for Thomas and for all "who have not seen and yet have believed" – faith in Jesus as the Anointed One and the only begotten Son of God, faith that brings eternal life in Jesus' name. We can be sure the Gospel writers have given us more than enough information to engender faith in our hearts, if only we'll believe despite not having been there to experience these things firsthand, to see them with our own eyes.

All four Gospels take up a mere 100 pages in my *ESV* Bible. According to author coach Daniel J. Tortora on the web, a "sweet spot" biography would be approximately nine chapters, 67,500 words, or 215 1.5-spaced pages.[11] Another writers' site suggests the average biography runs closer to nineteen chapters, 140,000 words, or 445 pages.[12] Yet another suggests between twelve to thirteen chapters, 95,000 words, or about 300 pages.[13] So our Gospels are indeed a very short biography for the greatest Man Who ever lived!

Interestingly, John himself only explored seven miracles in his book – turning water into wine at the wedding in Cana (John 2:1-11), healing the official's son "long distance" (for the Boomer, "remotely" for the Millennials, "virtually" for the Zoomers) (John 4:46-54), healing of the thirty-eight-year invalid at the Bethesda Pool (John 5:1-9), the feeding of more than 5,000 people with five loaves and two fish (John 6:1-5), walking on a rough sea (John 6:16-21), healing a man who was born blind (John 9:1-41), and

11 https://danieljtortora.com/blog/how-to-structure-biography-book
12 https://becomeawritertoday.com/average-length-of-a-book/
13 https://annerallen.com/2018/03/word-count-guidelines-by-genre/

raising Lazarus from the dead (John 11:1-44), not to mention His own resurrection enacted by His Father and Holy Spirit. John himself considered these signs, these miracles, sufficient to engender faith.

For those who might need a little extra convincing, let me remind you of other signs and miracles that Jesus performed in His earthly ministry as alluded to by Johann Albrecht Bengel in his *Gnomon* commentary on John 20:31: He purified the Temple – twice; He removed Peter's mother-in-law's fever; He cleansed ten lepers; He healed the centurion's paralyzed servant; He restrained and cast out demons on numerous occasions; He healed diseases and maladies that had lasted for years; he restored the sight of several blind people, including one man who had been born blind; He restored a withered hand; in addition to Lazarus, He raised both the synagogue ruler's twelve-year old daughter and the Nainian widow's son back to life; He commanded the wind and sea to be calm, and they obeyed; He commanded fish to leap into nets – twice; He also, at another time, miraculously fed over 4,000 people; He gave both the Twelve and the Seventy power over sickness, maladies, and demons; He cursed a fig tree to never bear fruit again; He merely spoke, "I am He," and an entire company of soldiers fell to the ground; He healed Malchus' ear; He occasionally healed entire crowds of people; and as we will yet see in the next Word, He prepared a miraculous breakfast by the Sea of Galilee.[14]

---

14 https://biblehub.com/commentaries/john/20-31.htm

MICHAEL A. SALSBURY

For Further Contemplation and Discussion:

When you contemplate Jesus in His glorified body during the forty days He spent on earth before His ascension, what thoughts and questions do you have? How do you imagine life will be in your glorified body?

Do you suppose Thomas followed through on his adamant insistence to touch Jesus' wounds, or did he content himself with merely seeing? Why or why not?

THE EIGHT *FIRST* WORDS OF CHRIST

Do you relate to Thomas and his doubts in your own faith journey, or are you more like John the Beloved, believing easily even when you don't understand? Explain.

Which miracles in the Gospel most strengthen your faith to believe, even though you didn't see them personally? Why those in particular?

CHAPTER EIGHT

Word Six

"Bring some of the fish…come and have breakfast…
If you love me, feed and tend my lambs, young sheep,
and sheep…Follow Me!"

THE APOSTLE JOHN, John the Evangelist, John the Beloved very much seems to have ended his book with verses 30 & 31 of chapter 20… but wait! There's more! Prepublication, John decided there was one other appearance of Jesus, one other encounter, one more Word he needed to add before releasing his Gospel into the world. It's a beautiful, idyllic fish story that hearkens back to the two sets of brothers' origins as fishermen – Peter and Andrew, and James and John – before they met Jesus and brings their lives full circle now that Jesus has succeeded in making them all "fishers of men." All that John had written before was designed for that purpose: to catch men in the nets of the Kingdom and bring them to faith in "Jesus' boat." This addendum, however, was added as a personal note, to clear up a rumor that persists even today concerning John himself and Jesus. This account and this Word appear only in John's Gospel.

The setting is the Sea of Tiberius, better known to us as the Sea of Galilee. Remember, Jesus had told Mary Magdalene and the angels had told the other women that Jesus would meet His disciples in Galilee. Apparently sometime after eight days of being cooped up in a room together in Jerusalem, cowering in fear of a Jewish persecution that was yet to come, the disciples decided to take Jesus up on His instruction; and they'd headed back to their Galilean roots. Away from Jerusalem and the confines of the city, they apparently didn't feel the need to stick so closely together, and they began other pursuits while waiting for Jesus to appear.

Verse 2 of chapter 21 tells us, "Simon Peter, Thomas (called the Twin), Nathanael of Cana in Galilee, the sons of Zebedee, and two others of his disciples were together." Of course, we could speculate all day about which other two disciples were with them – Andrew, Peter's brother, is conspicuous by his absence; and we must remember that there were many more disciples than the Twelve at this point (perhaps Cleopas and Friend were among them) – but we would be no closer to an answer. "Simon Peter said to them, 'I am going fishing.' They said to him, 'We will go with you.' They went out and got into the boat, but that night they caught nothing." We will not castigate Peter, James, John, and the others for doing what came naturally to them: Jesus did not condemn them for returning to what they knew to occupy their time while they waited, nor should we. We could remark that they caught nothing and presume some meaning behind that to be a lack of blessing on their effort, but we've been in these waters, literally, before in His story. Good storytellers merely call this "great foreshadowing" and move on.

"Just as day was breaking, Jesus stood on the shore; yet the disciples did not know that it was Jesus. Jesus said to them, 'Children, do you have any fish?'" According to Ellicott, the Greek word translated "children" here is closer to a coach or foreman referring to his grown men as "boys," to which Peter might have replied, "Boys?!? Do you call the Sea of Galilee a puddle?"

"They answered him, 'No.' We can still hear their exhaustion in that one-word answer.

"He said to them, 'Cast the net on the right side of the boat, and you will find some.'" This so-far "stranger" has not yet given any credentials that would suggest He knows anything about fishing, and this instruction certainly didn't lend credence to such knowledge: doubtlessly, the men had cast their nets on *both* sides (and ends!) of the boat in hopes of catching fish overnight; and even if they had for some unknown reason cast their nets only on the left side of the boat, why would a boat's width make any difference in catching fish? Surely soon, someone's going to wake up and realize this is Jesus giving them commands! Again, they've cast these nets before…

"So they cast it, and now they were not able to haul it in because of the quantity of fish. That disciple whom Jesus loved [This is how John referred to himself throughout his Gospel…] therefore said to Peter, 'It is the Lord!'" Thank you, Captain Obvious!

"When Simon Peter heard that it was the Lord, he put on his outer garment, for he was stripped for work, and threw himself into the sea. The other disciples came in the boat, dragging the net full of fish, for they were not far from the land but about a hundred yards off." Now, I don't know about you, but I take clothes *off* rather than put clothes *on* when I'm about to go for a swim. Obviously, Peter put on his cloak to come to shore and get to Jesus fully clothed out of respect rather than convenience. He had the length of a football field to cover and much of it may have been shallow, but notice this was also an effort to get to Christ *before* everyone else. Impetuous Peter wades again!

"When they got out on land, they saw a charcoal fire in place, with fish laid out on it, and bread." Here is the miraculous breakfast I mentioned at the very end of the last chapter. "What makes it so miraculous?" you may ask, "Fish and bread is a reasonable breakfast in the Mediterranean Diet." Perhaps, but look more closely. The fire is not freshly built but already a "charcoal fire" as if it has been burning a long time; yet the disciples did not notice a fire on shore through all the long night they had labored not more than a hundred yards away. (You may later be reminded that it was a charcoal fire by which Peter denied Jesus three times, and it will be beside this charcoal fire that Peter will be restored three times to his new ministry.) The fish and bread appear hot and fresh and ready to eat, but they had not smelled the aroma of the meal wafting out to them on the lake, nor had they seen another fisherman fishing offshore or anyone making bread for that matter. This is indeed another miracle of loaves and fishes! (I love my fried fish and hushpuppies, but I'm not gonna lie: I kind of hope He applies this power to steak and baked potatoes in heaven!)

"Jesus said to them, 'Bring some of the fish that you have just caught.' [*i.e.* 'I've only made enough for us to get started, but this is obviously not enough for seven men who have been working hard all night.'] So Simon Peter went aboard and hauled the net ashore, full of large fish, 153 of them. And although there were so many, the net was not torn." Despite many human efforts to attach some significance to the number "153," I personally find no credible reason to consider it beyond the fact that it was merely an enormous and specific number of fish and should have broken their nets; but it didn't.

"Jesus said to them, 'Come and have breakfast.' Not one of the disciples dared ask him, 'Who are you?' They knew it was the Lord." Once again, the disciples recognized Him around a meal. Was there in this encounter some modicum of disguise in Jesus' appearance? It appears at least to be somehow, slightly questionably Him, enough for the disciples to have *reason* to question but not the courage to do so. Certainly, the miracle of the fish and the breakfast would indicate it was Him, for who else could do such things so, if there were reason to question, it would have lain in His appearance or voice. "So Jesus came and took the bread and gave it to them, and so with the fish." Breakfast! "This was now the third time that Jesus was revealed to the disciples [as a group] after he was raised from the dead," but this encounter is leisurely and lasts much longer than is recorded of the other two.

Now begins an extended Word with Peter. When they had finished breakfast, bellies full of fish and bread, satisfied and leisurely, Jesus asked Peter to take a stroll with him on the beach; and Jesus said to him, "Simon, son of Jonah, do you love Me more than these?" First, let us notice that Jesus uses Peter's given name, Simon Jonahson, if you will, rather than the nickname "Peter" (*Cephas*, "rock" or "stone") which He Himself had given to him as they began their journey together. Jesus is purposefully taking Peter back to the beginning to recommission him for ministry. Second, let us note that Jesus uses the Greek *agape* (pronounce *ah gah' pay*) that we translate here as *love*, that self-sacrificing, other-focused, deepest kind of love that God possesses for us and demonstrated to us in sending His Son to die for our sins. This distinction becomes important as we proceed through this conversation. Here are several ways in which Jesus' question to Peter might be interpreted:

First, do you love Me more than you love these… whom? These *people*, friends and colleagues of yours, more than Thomas and Nathanael, more than your cousins and fellow fishermen James and John, more than your brother Andrew or perhaps even your wife? This question hearkens us back to Jesus' teaching in Matthew 10:37: "Whoever loves father or mother more than me is not worthy of me, and whoever loves son or daughter more than me is not worthy of me."

Second, do you love Me more than you love these… what? These *things*, these boats and nets and fishing implements, this occupation of fishing and the money to be gained by it? Are you willing to give all that up for the ministry to which I am calling you, this fishing of men I would have you do, and more? You've had a taste of the life I expect you to lead. Would you return to your former occupation, to life as you knew it before you met Me?

Third, as a comparison: do you love Me more than these *other men love Me*? Remember, Peter had claimed in Matthew 26:33, "Though they all fall away because of You, I will never fall away" and in John 13:37, "I will lay down my life for You"; yet he had subsequently denied the Lord three times, and His colleagues knew he had done so.

Finally, I will mention that the same ambiguity lies in the original language as in our English translations so perhaps Jesus intended Peter to consider *all* these things in His reply.

No matter how Peter understood the question, his response was straightforward and simple: "He said to Him, 'Yes, Lord; You know that I love You.'" Peter it seems here, perhaps having learned his lesson of being so cocksure (pun intended) of himself and his love for his Lord, knows better than to go so far that he has learned to *agape* Jesus so he more humbly and certainly more honestly answers, "You know that I *phileo* (*fi lay' oh*) You: I love You with a brotherly affection that cannot be denied." As eminent Nineteenth Century American theologian Albert Barnes writes in his *Notes* on this verse, "It is not the most confident pretensions that constitute the highest proof of love to Christ; and the happiest and best state of feeling is when we can with humility, yet with confidence, look to the Lord Jesus and say, 'Thou knowest that I love thee.'"[15] Peter had finally learned to let Christ be the judge of his heart.

"[Jesus] said to him, 'Feed My lambs,'" meaning most certainly the youngest and most defenseless of the sheep (the original Greek is better interpreted "littlest lambs" – certainly the children, the babes in Christ, those who are easy to love because of their cuteness and *joie de vivre*, but also the "runts" of the litter, those who need to be bottle-fed and snuggled just to be kept alive). Remember that Jesus said in Matthew 19:14, "'Let the little children come to me and do not hinder them, for to such belongs

---

15 https://biblehub.com/commentaries/john/21-15.htm

the kingdom of heaven.'" Of what does this feeding (the Greek word used is *boskein*) of the young and defenseless consist? Peter would later write in I Peter 2:2, "Like newborn infants, long for the pure spiritual milk, that by it you may grow up into salvation." The *King James Version* includes milk "of the Word" (not in the original Greek), those essentials of the Gospel and basic elements of the Christian walk by faith that are foundational to living a Kingdom life.

"[Jesus] said to him a second time, 'Simon, son of Jonah, do you love Me?'

"He said to Him, 'Yes, Lord; You know that I love You.'

"He said to him, 'Tend my sheep.'"

This second exchange is exactly the same as the first, except in Christ's response to Peter. The word translated "tend" here includes feeding (the Greek word here is *poimainein*) but also the ideas of guiding, watching, and defending the sheep, the word used here referring not to lambs nor to mature sheep but to "little sheep," young sheep, an adolescent sheep, if you will. While the younger lambs need primarily to be instructed in the basics of being part of the flock, they need less guidance because they remain close to their mothers and cannot travel great distances; the more adolescent sheep need less but more detailed instruction as they grow and more and more guidance and protection from their foolish propensity to wander and stray. How perfectly are we compared to sheep!

"He said to him the third time, 'Simon, son of Jonah, do you love Me?' This time, Jesus uses Peter's word for love, *phileo*, rather than the *agape* that He had used previously. I do not believe, as some scholars would suggest, that Jesus is sincerely questioning Peter's friendship although He is obviously asking Peter to question it. Does Peter sincerely, as he has twice claimed, "*phileo*" Jesus? Does he sincerely love Him as a friend or brother? I believe this was Jesus' concession to Peter's humility not to claim a love higher than he knew he could truthfully confess. I believe Jesus asked Peter for three separate testimonies or avowals in order to establish his love for Jesus going forward, despite the past, beyond all doubt.

"Peter was grieved because He said to him the third time, 'Do you love Me?'" I mean, wouldn't you be grieved if your best friend in all the world asked you if you loved him or her three times inside of a minute and a half? As best as Peter knew his heart, he knew he loved Jesus with all of it. The three-fold question implied that Jesus might doubt that love, and Peter knew he had given cause for that doubt so his reply became all the more impassioned.

"And he said to Him, 'Lord, you *know* everything; You *know* that I love You'" [emphasis added]. Again, our English language fails us in understanding the nuance of Peter's passionate reply. The Greek uses two different words for our English word *know*. The first, *oidas*, is the word Peter has been using all along and refers to Jesus' supernatural intuition. The second, *ginóskeis*, refers to Jesus' experience and discernment. "Please, Jesus. You're omniscient! We've been together for three years. Doesn't Your experience in our relationship vouch for my sincerity? You *know* me! If I'm insincere in the least, you would know." How does Peter know that Jesus knows everything? Again, Bengel comes to our rescue with a list of many of the demonstrations of Jesus' omniscience in the Gospels. According to John, over the course of His ministry, Jesus knew who Simon was, the mind and actions of Nathanael, what is in the heart of every man, the relationships of the Samaritan woman at the well, the treachery of Judas and of others, the death of Lazarus, when His appointed time had come, Peter's denial, the disciples' desire to question Him, and those things which would come upon Him and their consummation. According to the Synoptic Gospels, Jesus knew the thoughts of men; what Solomon's clothes looked like in comparison to the lilies of the field; what Sodom, Tyre, and Sidon would have done had they seen Jesus' miracles; His own Passion ahead of time; the destruction of Jerusalem; and the circumstances which would accompany His entrance into Jerusalem and the Passover Feast (among others).[16]

"Jesus said to him, 'Feed My sheep.'" While there is some question concerning the word for sheep used here and its precise meaning, traditionally it is seen as older sheep so that we have a progression from lamb to young sheep to mature sheep in Jesus' commission to Peter. Peter's new role as shepherd of the people of God was to feed, nurture, guide, and protect the entire family of God, cradle to grave. That's a pretty daunting task for any pastor.

Bible scholars have made much of connecting Jesus' asking Peter if he loved Him three times with Peter's having denied Jesus three times, which smacks to me a bit of Jesus rubbing Peter's nose in his sin and all that analogy implies. As Matthew Henry says in his *Concise Commentary*, "Every remembrance of past sins, even pardoned sins, renews the sorrow of a true penitent."[17] I don't think that's what Jesus is about here. God can certainly restore a penitent sinner to faithful service without forcing him to remember over

---

16 https://biblehub.com/commentaries/john/21-17.htm
17 https://biblehub.com/commentaries/john/21-16.htm

and over the sin that broke their fellowship. I much prefer Jesus repeating His question to Peter three times with the very Hebrew mindset of repetition for emphasis. This is especially true in Hebrew poetry, and one need look no further than to the longest chapter in the Bible, Psalm 119, for proof of that. We find Jesus using repetition throughout His teaching whenever He uses "Truly, truly, I say to you…" The word He is using is related to the Hebrew "Amen! Amen!" or "So be it, so be it!" He is essentially saying, "I have this not only on good authority but also by firsthand knowledge." The repetition is emphasizing the truth of the matter. Jesus repeats His questions and responses to firmly cement His intention for Peter's *future*, not past, in *Peter's* mind and heart.

In this particular setting, it is clear that Jesus is calling Peter from his original calling of a fisherman and subsequently *fisher of men* to "shepherd" and pastor of the flock Jesus is leaving in His care. Fishermen and shepherds have very different relationships to the animals with which they work. Fishermen catch fish for the purpose of consuming them themselves and selling them to others to eat. It is a labor of sustenance for the *fisherman* and death for the fish. Shepherds, on the other hand, tend and feed their sheep with an eye to reproduction, wool production, milk production (in the case of goats), and the overall life of the sheep. It is a labor of sustenance for both the *sheep **and*** the shepherd!

The prerequisite for anyone to be a pastor, a shepherd of the people of God, is a firm and unshakable love for the Great Shepherd, for Jesus Himself. He prefers the pastor love Him with *His* love, that *agape,* self-sacrificing, deeply intimate love with which He loves us; but if, out of humble honesty, all that can be truly mustered at a given moment

THE EIGHT *FIRST* WORDS OF CHRIST

is *phileo*, the friendship and brotherhood that only comes through common trials and experiences, that will have to do. I am reminded as I'm sure Peter was of Jesus' teaching in John 10 about Jesus being the Good Shepherd (one of the seven great "I am" statements in John's Gospel). In verses 5-6, in speaking of His flock, Jesus said, "'A stranger they will not follow, but they will flee from him, for they do not know the voice of strangers.' This figure of speech Jesus used with them, but they did not understand what he was saying to them." Of course not: they were fishermen, not shepherds! The pastor must love the Good Shepherd well enough that there is something of His voice in theirs when they minister to the sheep. John goes on in verses 12-13 to talk about mere "hired hands": "He who is a hired hand and not a shepherd, who does not own the sheep, sees the wolf coming and leaves the sheep and flees, and the wolf snatches them and scatters them. He flees because he is a hired hand and cares nothing for the sheep." A true shepherd must also truly love the sheep.

My dad grew up on the farm, and when I was a teenager, we had a barn and sheep on our property, primarily to keep half the acreage "mown." The sheep were Dad's domain, and he rarely asked my brother or me to have any part in their care, which was handy as I really had no interest in sheep at that time. When Dad went to the barn, the sheep would always come in from the pasture, often without him having to call them; but one sharp "Sheep!" in my dad's high-pitched voice was all it took to set them running to him. My brother and I could stand at the fence and cry "Sheep!" all day with not so much as a glance from the sheep! One week in the summer following my graduation from college, however, the family took a vacation, and I was unable to go along so it fell to me to care for the sheep. Dad had shown me how and what to feed them; but initially I had trouble getting them to come close, even when they saw me pour the grain into the trough. I tried imitating my dad when calling and talking to them, and they would cock their ears and stare at me, knowing I wasn't Dad and yet "there's something about him that reminds us of our shepherd" could be read in their eyes. Still, they initially would not approach the trough until I left the barn, muttering, "Well, I guess they'll eat when they get hungry enough…" Before the week was up, however, they were coming up to the trough right away and even allowing a few pats on the head. (Never mind that I almost accidentally killed them because I didn't remember the difference between oats and wheat, but that's a story for another day….)

Having secured Peter in His love for Him and his new role as First Pastor to the Flock of God (which happily happened to include the occasional fishing trip for people), Jesus chose to give Peter a glimpse of his earthly end. Verse 18-19a says, "'Truly, truly, I say to you, when you were young, you used to dress yourself and walk wherever you wanted, but when you are old, you will stretch out your hands, and another will dress you and carry you where you do not want to go.' (This He said to show by what kind of death he was to glorify God.)" We might think this a rather macabre and morbid way in which to demonstrate One's omniscience; but Jesus was reassuring Peter that, despite his failures and because of this great shepherding service he was about to render to His Lord, he would be allowed to follow His Lord in crucifixion and a martyr's death. Perhaps, in keeping with Peter's impetuosity to the very end, it was this very prophecy that caused Peter to determine that he would *not* count himself worthy to suffer as Jesus had: while nowhere recounted in Scripture, tradition says Peter insisted on being crucified upside down in Rome, so as not to be crucified in the same manner as His Lord and Savior, and that this happened some thirty-four years after Jesus spoke this Word. Before his death, Peter would write about the importance of suffering with and for Christ (I Peter 4:12-19). Paul says in Philippians 1:29 it is a gift both to believe in Jesus and to suffer for Him.

Verse 19b says, "And after saying this, he said to him, 'Follow me.'" In the end, nothing has changed one whit for Peter. Jesus' final commission to Peter is the same as His first: "Follow me." This is all our Savior ever asks of any of us, not as some commandant ordering us to "fall in, get in line, and march" but as the Great Shepherd leading His flock to the still waters and green pastures in God's Kingdom. Follow Me!

Of course, this is impetuous Peter we are talking about here so saying to him "Follow me" merely one time will not likely be enough. John continues the tale of their beach walk in verse 20: "Peter turned and saw the disciple whom Jesus loved following them, the one who also had leaned back against him during the supper and had said, 'Lord, who is it that is going to betray you?'" As already mentioned, John often referred to himself as "the disciple whom Jesus loved," and here he goes further to identify himself as the one whom Peter had asked to ask Jesus who would betray Him at the Last Supper. John didn't want anyone to miss the fact that he is speaking about himself here. It is also ironic to note that John was *doing* the very thing Jesus had just commanded Peter to do: he was *following* Jesus (and

Peter). John was at the ready to serve his Master's will: "they also serve who stand [or walk] and wait."

John goes on: "When Peter saw him, he said to Jesus, 'Lord, what about this man?'" In light of his present conversation with Jesus, Peter could be asking many questions in this one: "If I'm to be the shepherd of the flock, what is this man's job going to be?" or "If I'm to be martyred by crucifixion, how will this man die?" or "Where does this guy fall in the pecking order now?"

Why did Peter ask about John? I think we need look no further than the disciples' recurring argument about which of them was the greatest. When Jesus first caught them in the argument in Matthew 18, He taught them the lesson of becoming humble like a child, of becoming the least of all, and of welcoming children and thereby welcoming the Father Who had sent His Son to them. Later, as they were nearing Jericho on their final journey to Jerusalem, Jesus' Aunt Salome, Mrs. Zebedee, had come with her sons James and John and knelt before Jesus, asking him to grant a favor, "whatever we ask," without telling Him what the favor was. (Entrap much?) When Jesus asked what they wanted, Salome and Sons asked that James and John be allowed to sit, one on Jesus's right and one on His left, in God's Kingdom. Even though Jesus replied that this privilege was not His to grant (presumably rather His Father's), when the other disciples heard about it, they were indignant with James and John for even making the request in the first place, probably because they were simply jealous not to have thought to ask the boon for themselves first.

Perhaps Peter now had finally answered the question, in his own mind anyway, of who was the greatest: "*C'est moi!*" Seeing that Jesus had evidently selected him to be the leader of the sheep, what position could He possibly have left to give to poor John, whom Peter knew the Lord to love at least as well if not better than He loved him. O the machinations of the human heart! He may also have been wondering, having just been told he would experience crucifixion as his end, if John would be martyred in a similar fashion.

"Jesus said to him, 'If it is My will that he remain until I come, what is that to you? You follow Me!'" If there were more to add to this Word Six, I believe it would be "Follow Me… and mind your own business!" Here is a rebuke similar to what Jesus gave to Martha, the Worker, when she asked Him to shoo her sister Mary, the Worshiper, away from His feet to get the meal on the table. In light of the weighty work Jesus has just commissioned Peter to do as Chief Undershepherd and the martyrdom he would someday face, it was hard for Peter to imagine that Jesus would not have something similar in mind for his "brother" and fellow disciple John, whom Jesus loved at least as well as him if not better; but Peter was not to make this any of his concern.

History and tradition tell us that John, as probably the youngest of the disciples, was the last to die, living almost to the end of the first century. He supposedly died peacefully in Ephesus, the only one of the Twelve not to suffer *death* by martyrdom, although he *was* martyred. In addition to imprisonment with Peter and prior to banishment to Patmos, tradition says that Emperor Domitian sentenced John to be boiled in oil *but* that John emerged unscathed from the experience, causing the entire audience in the Colosseum that day to convert to Christianity! In fact, it was because he couldn't kill him that Domitian banished him to Patmos.

"So the saying spread abroad among the brothers and sisters that this disciple was not to die; yet Jesus did not say to him that he was not to die, but, 'If it is my will that he remain until I come, what is that to you?'" While tradition suggests that John was released from Patmos by Nerva, Domitian's successor, and returned to Ephesus to live out his days and was the only one of the Twelve to die a peaceful death sometime between A.D. 98 and 120, this "saying" exists to this day. When the Catholics exhumed what is presumed to be John's tomb near ancient Ephesus to remove his bones to a reliquary, none were found, prompting the notion that John's body had been assumed into heaven. Or had he never been buried, indeed never *died*, in the first place? Some, however, suggest, based on John's consumption of the little scroll on Patmos during the Revelation, that he remains alive and will be one of the two witnesses during the seven-year Tribulation period.[18] "Then the voice that I had heard from heaven spoke to me again, saying, 'Go, take the scroll that is open in the hand of the angel who is standing on the sea and on the land.' So I went to the angel and told him to give me the little scroll. And he said to me, 'Take and eat it; it will make your stomach bitter, but it will be sweet as honey in your mouth.' And I took the little scroll from the hand of the angel and ate it. It was sweet as honey in my mouth; but when I had eaten it, my stomach was made bitter. And I was told, 'You must again prophesy about many peoples and nations and languages and kings' (Revelation 10:8-11)." The thinking goes, since there is no record of John

---

18 https://christianity.stackexchange.com/questions/1123/what-happened-to-the-apostle-john-after-the-biblical-account-of-his-life-ends

yet making this prophecy, he will yet do so sometime in the future. Of course, like Enoch or Moses or Elijah, other names that are often put forward as a possible "witness" of the Two in the last days, there is mystery enshrouding John's death. You may say, "Yes, but John here is refuting the very notion…"; but don't we know prophets have been wrong about their own fates before – John the Baptist said he was not Elijah, after all. To think that John the Beloved may still be drawing breath somewhere on the face of the earth for the past two thousand years, albeit with a perpetual bellyache, patiently waiting to unleash this long-brewing prophecy upon the ears of the earth is intriguing, fascinating, and fantastic fiction fodder to be sure.

John finishes his Gospel with this sixth word of Christ out the tomb. "This is the disciple who is bearing witness about these things, and who has written these things, and we know that his testimony is true. Now there are also many other things that Jesus did. Were every one of them to be written, I suppose that the world itself could not contain the books that would be written" … or that are yet to be written…

For Further Contemplation and Discussion:

What interests, hobbies, or occupation did you have prior to meeting Jesus that remain permissible for you to do anytime you are waiting for an assignment from Him.

I responded to Christ's call to full-time ministry at a burned-down bonfire at Bible camp. Do you have any "charcoal fire" experiences with the Lord? Explain and share.

THE EIGHT *FIRST* WORDS OF CHRIST

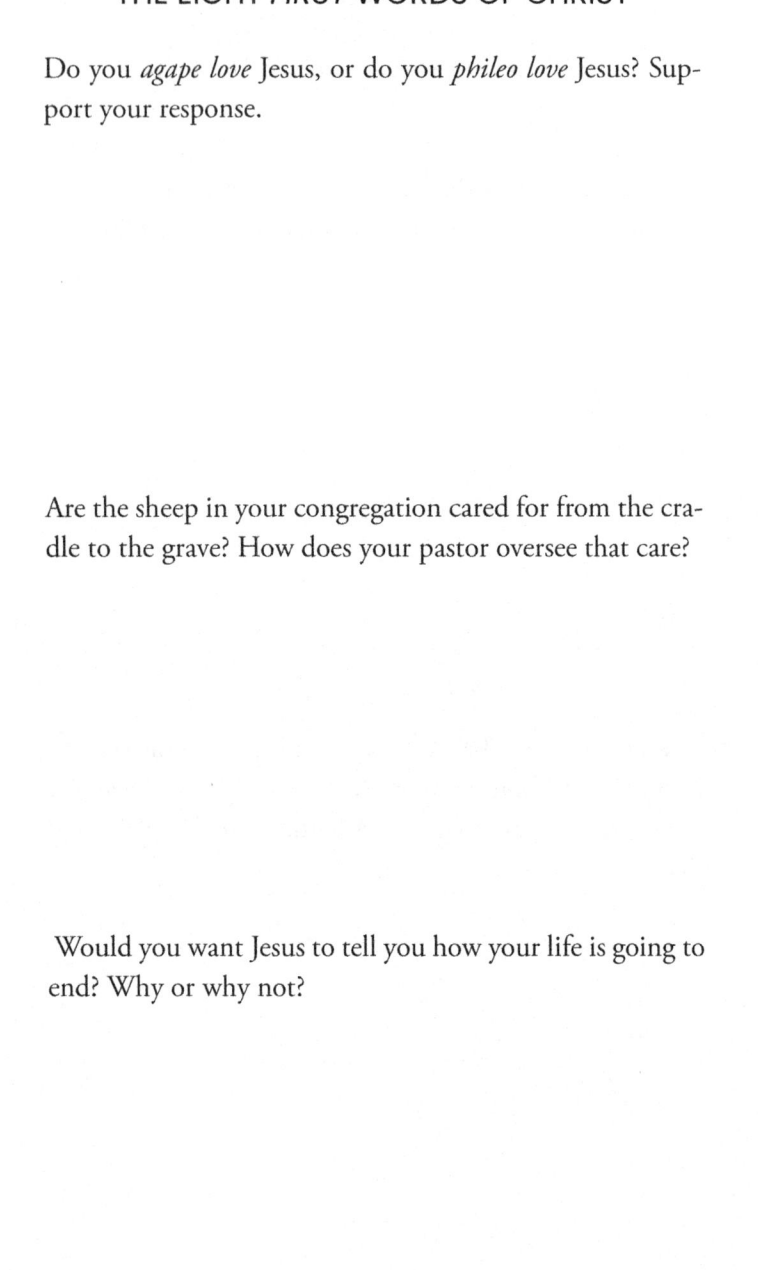

Do you *agape love* Jesus, or do you *phileo love* Jesus? Support your response.

Are the sheep in your congregation cared for from the cradle to the grave? How does your pastor oversee that care?

Would you want Jesus to tell you how your life is going to end? Why or why not?

CHAPTER NINE

Word Seven

"Go! Make disciples, baptizing them and teaching them…
Lo, I am with you always, even unto the end of the age."

Until this point in the writing of this book, I labored under the impression that there were two separate events in which Jesus commissioned His disciples, one taking place on a Galilean mount and one taking place back in the upper room in Jerusalem; but in the actual writing, I found myself mistaken. Matthew and Mark record Christ's "super appearance" in Galilee, the major one for which I believe all along He has been preparing His followers, and the Apostle Paul corroborates this meeting in I Corinthians 15:6. The events described by Dr. Luke, both in his Gospel and in the Book of Acts, I discovered rather to be part of Word Four already discussed and the infamous Word Eight yet to come. I will also mention Jesus' appearance to his half-brother James, the content to which we are not made privy.

THE EIGHT *FIRST* WORDS OF CHRIST

On the night before Christ's crucifixion, after the disciples had begun their last supper together with Jesus, after He had washed their feet and identified Judas as the betrayer, and after He had given His "new commandment" that they love one another, just before He predicts Peter's denial, Matthew and Mark begin setting the stage for Jesus' resurrection and this meeting in Galilee. We'll let Matthew do the talking in 26:31-32: "Then Jesus said to them, 'You will all fall away because of me this night. For it is written [in Zechariah 13:7], "I will strike the shepherd, and the sheep of the flock will be scattered." But after I am raised up, I will go before you to Galilee.'" This is the moment to which both the angels and Jesus referred when they each separately told the women to tell the disciples to meet Him in Galilee as He'd said. It must have been a meeting place well known to both Jesus and his followers, and I can think of no other mountain more familiar to them all than the one upon which He first appointed the Twelve and afterward preached His "Sermon on the Mount." They already knew this place could accommodate a large gathering of people, and I believe this is the event of which Paul spoke in I Corinthians 15:6 in which "he appeared to more than five hundred brothers at one time, most of whom are still alive, though some have fallen asleep." Since, as in the feedings of the 5,000 and 4,000, only the number of men is mentioned here and Paul does say "more than five hundred brothers at one time," I think we can safely say this was a gathering of upwards to 1,500 or more followers of Christ.

Matthew goes on to give us Christ's Word in Matthew 28:17-20, "And when they saw Him, they worshiped Him; but some doubted. And Jesus came and said to them, 'All authority in heaven and on earth has been given to me. Go therefore and make disciples of all nations, baptizing them in[to] the name of the Father and of the Son and of the Holy Spirit, teaching them to observe all that I have commanded you. And behold, I am with you always, to the end of the age.'"

To worship means "to ascribe worth": to proclaim something's importance, to establish value. We worship things by attaching a monetary value to them every day, but even that value changes from moment to moment: a brand new window-unit air conditioner may be had for anywhere from $200-700 today, but a used one might be picked up for $25-100; however, neither one is of much value at all in the midst of a Michigan winter but any one of them becomes priceless on a hot, muggy day, as long as it works! What value would you place on the Redeemer of your soul, the Man Who saved you from hell and damnation and has gone to prepare a place for you in heaven to be with Him for the rest of eternity, your Bridegroom forever? If I ever rise from my face at His feet, it will be too soon.

"But some doubted." This is why I believe this was a meeting of much more than just the eleven disciples that Matthew includes because we know that, by this point in the narrative, not even Thomas is doubting Jesus' resurrection. No one suffers martyrdom for something they doubt in the least. By the time Paul got around to writing I Corinthians, some of the five hundred who had seen Jesus that day had already died. I pray they did not die in doubt! Can you imagine? Doubting the One and Only One Whom God has ever yet raised to life again to live forever, defeating Sin, Death, and the Grave, Whom you can see and

THE EIGHT *FIRST* WORDS OF CHRIST

hear standing right in front of you? Doubting He Who has proved, "My Father has given me all authority in heaven and on earth," even authority over death! This is not a Man to be doubted!

So, what is the Word, then, O Universal Authority? What are we to do? What say ye?

"Go."

Status quo be damned! Stay? No way. Move! Leave! Get out of Dodge! Journey on! Onward and upward! This world is not my home: I'm just a-passin' through. This has ever been God's commission to the human race. All the way back to Adam and Eve in the Garden in Genesis 1:28, "…God blessed them. And God said to them, "Be fruitful and multiply and fill the earth and subdue it…" How could they fill the earth if they did not move away from home, from the epicenter? When Adam and Eve chose to eat of the forbidden fruit and fell short of God's glory, God *sent* them away from the Garden so they wouldn't eat from the Tree of Life and have to live forever in their fallen state. Genesis 3:24 says He "drove out the man." Go! After Cain killed his brother Abel, he became a "fugitive and a wanderer." Go! After Noah, built the Ark, God said in Genesis 7:1, "*Go* into the ark…," and when the earth had finally dried out from the Flood, God said Genesis 8:16, "*Go* out from the ark…." Go, float above the chaos in safety for a while, and then go some more. In Genesis 9:1, God told Noah's family once again to "fill the earth," to move away from the Ark of safety, away from the epicenter. In Genesis 10, we learn of all the nations that descended from Noah up until the Tower of Babel in Genesis 11, where God again had to confuse the languages of the earth in order to "disperse them over the face of the earth"? Go! Finally, what was God's first word to Abram when He called him to follow Him by faith? "*Go* from your country and your kindred and your father's house to the land that I will show you (Genesis 12:1)." Go!

Why this emphasis on going? I believe there are several good reasons always to choose to "go." First, we are fulfilling God's original mandate to "fill the earth." As long as there are uninhabited frontiers, we are called to move away from the populace and into the wide-open spaces. Second, when we go, we grow. Change challenges us and stimulates growth. This from a man who has moved twenty-one times in forty years of marriage. Third, going back to the Fall in the Garden, this fallen, broken world is no longer hospitable to us. We are merely sojourners here, longing to get to our eternal home, a place made for us as surely as the original Garden was made for us. Travel reminds us that we are aliens in this world, foreigners, traveling to a better land. Fourth, to go is a demonstration of faith. The known, even if unhealthy for us, is comfortable; the unknown is a scary place, even if it is ultimately better for us than where we are. When God tells us to go, He is inviting us to trust Him in the going and not knowing, to trust Him instead of other people or even ourselves, to trust Him that "there" will be better than "here," not because the grass is greener but because that's where He's going to be with you. Finally, we are fulfilling this "Great Commission" to "Go!"

But what are we to be doing as we go? God doesn't want us merely running like rats on a wheel; we don't go for the sake of going. In Word 7, Jesus' imperative is to make disciple of all nations. See how this echoes that original mandate back in Genesis 1:28 to fill the earth? The gospel of Jesus Christ is all-inclusive; it is meant for every tribe and every nation of the human race. How do we "make disciples?" The same way Jesus did: attract people to Him by being loving and caring, by becoming like Him, and then by calling them to follow Him in His way of life.

Making disciples is a two-fold process. Once a person makes the decision to follow Jesus, we are to "baptize them in the name of the Father and of the Son and of the Holy Spirit." New converts to discipleship choose to be baptized for several reasons. First, baptism is a sign of repentance, a sign that the new believer is not only choosing to be like Jesus but is also turning away and repenting from his sinful ways of living. John the Baptist's baptism was a baptism of repentance. This is why he called the Pharisees and religious leaders of Jesus' day "a brood of snakes and vipers" because they didn't see themselves as sinful in any way. Supposedly, they had no sin from which to repent and so refused to participate in John's baptism, but that was obviously wrong because we *all* have sinned and fallen short of God's glory (Romans 3:23). Second, Jesus set an example for us to be baptized because He, the only sinless human being to ever walk this earth, *did* participate in John's baptism of repentance, despite John's protest to the contrary (Matthew 3:14). Third, baptism is a public statement of our turning away from our sins and identifying with Jesus. It is a public witness and testimony to our belief in Christ. Fourth, it is a public vow, not unlike a wedding vow, in which we "take the name" of Father, Son, and Holy Spirit upon ourselves. Much like a bride traditionally takes her husband's name as her own, so the Bride of Christ, the Church, and each individual member of the Church, takes His Name, becomes known as "Christian," in the sacrament of baptism. We are baptized into the Name of the

Triune God: Father, Son, and Holy Spirit. Finally, it is a symbolic picture of what happens in our salvation. Our sins, from which we have turned away, were nailed to His cross, and we are "buried in the likeness of His death and raised in the likeness of His resurrection."

The second part of making disciples involves teaching new believers "to obey *everything* I [Jesus] have commanded you [emphasis added]." Well, now, *that* seems a little daunting, doesn't it? How can I teach someone else to obey every single word Jesus ever commanded us when I'm still having trouble applying it all and living it out on a consistent basis day after day? Good news! The night before He died, Jesus said this: "A new commandment I give to you, that you love one another: just as I have loved you, you also are to love one another. By this all people will know that you are my disciples, if you have love for one another (John 13:34-35)." This hearkens back to His answer to a Pharisaical lawyer who once asked Him, "Teacher, which is the greatest commandment in the Law?" And He said to him, "You shall love the Lord your God with all your heart and with all your soul and with all your mind. This is the great and first commandment. And a second is like it: You shall love your neighbor as yourself. On these two commandments depend all the Law and the Prophets. (Matthew 22:36-40)" If we teach other disciples to love God and to love others, we *are* teaching them to obey *everything* Jesus ever commanded. That is not to say that personal Bible reading, corporate Bible study, and public teaching of God's Word are not important in training believers in *how* to love God and love others and what it means to love God and love others, but still we are blessed to have a "finger-tip guide" to obedience at the ready at all times: love

God, love others. Until we know the answer to Charles Sheldon's "what would Jesus do?", we can simply ask the questions, "Am I loving God?" and "Am I loving others" to keep ourselves on the path of obedience.

That is not to mention the final failsafe He gives His followers on the mountain in Galilee: "And behold, I am with you always, to the end of the age." We are not left alone and to our own resources and devices (which would undoubtedly fail miserably) in this quest of teaching others to follow Jesus. Jesus promised to be with us to the end of this earthly life in the Person of His Holy Spirit. Again, we are reminded of His promise, after He has entered His Glory and sat down at the right hand of His Father to rule and intercede in prayer with His Father on our behalf, to send His Holy Spirit, His *Parakletos*, the One Who comes alongside to help, to comfort, to instruct, and to guide us into all Truth. He Himself remains with us even to this day to assist in this commission to make disciples of all nations. It is impossible for us *not* to succeed in this effort!

After Jesus appeared to the multitude on the mountain in Galilee, the Apostle Paul tells us He made a couple of other appearances: "Then he appeared to James, then to all the apostles" (I Corinthians 15:7). It is universally decided that the "James" to which Jesus appeared here is His oldest half-brother James, eldest son of Mary and Joseph (unless you are Catholic or Eastern Orthodox) and elder brother to Joses, Jude, Simon, and at least two or more unnamed sisters. James and his brothers are notorious in Scripture for being unsure of Jesus and His claims throughout His life. Early on in Jesus' ministry, Jesus's popularity grew to a point that, when He entered the place where He was staying, He and His disciples were so overrun by needy people that they couldn't even eat. When Mary and His half-brothers heard of it, "they went out to seize Him, for they were saying, 'He is out of his mind.'" Not exactly paragons of faith at that point! When they got to the house where Jesus was "beleaguered," they couldn't even get in to see Him; but when Jesus was told His family was outside asking for Him, His reply was, "Who is my mother, and who are my brothers? Here are my mother and brothers [referring to those gathered around Him listening] because whoever does God will, whoever hears God's Word and puts it into practice, is My brother and sister and mother." Not exactly an endearing response to His family's ears!

Later, as He was finishing His Galilean ministry, the final Feast of Tabernacles that Jesus would celebrate in His earthly ministry was drawing near; and Jesus knew the Jewish leadership in Jerusalem was already looking for a way to kill Him. "So his brothers and sisters said to him, 'Leave here and go to Judea, that your disciples also may see the works you are doing. For no one works in secret if he seeks to be known openly. *If* you do these things, show yourself to the world.' For not even his brothers and sisters believed in him [John 7:3-5, emphasis added]." Essentially, they were taunting Him: "Look, put up or shut up. *If* you're the miracle worker you claim to be (and we strongly suspect you are not), then get out there and do these miracles publicly in Jerusalem. No one who wants to be a celebrity stays in backwater Nazareth. You need to go to the Big Pomegranate, to Jerusalem, and make your mark on the world." Not one of them, James included, was speaking from a faith perspective.

Six months later, their big brother was dead, arrested by the Jewish council and crucified violently at the hands of the

THE EIGHT *FIRST* WORDS OF CHRIST

Romans. Three days later, there was a rumor that He had been raised from the dead; and the rumor didn't go away. Four and a half weeks later, over a thousand people claimed they saw Him and heard Him speak on a nearby Galilean mountain. Paul says, "Then He appeared to James."

We are told nothing of what is said in this appearance so we don't get another Word out of it at all, but the next thing we hear about half-brother James is that he has somehow become the first *leader* of the Jerusalem Church. Whatever Jesus said to his half-brother in this *one* encounter taught him as much or more than Peter and the Zebedee boys picked up in three *years* of following Jesus!

For Further Contemplation and Discussion:

What value would you place on the Redeemer of your soul, the Man Who saved you from hell and damnation and has gone to prepare a place for you in heaven to be with Him for the rest of eternity, your Bridegroom forever?

You will note that I have skirted Mark's account of the Great Commission completely in a bid for unity in the Body of Christ, being aware of the controversy over the validity of the passage and the differences in theologies that have been based on the passage. Please study Mark 16:15-18 and allow the Holy Spirit to instruct you concerning this passage.

THE EIGHT *FIRST* WORDS OF CHRIST

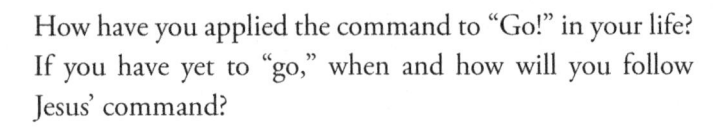

How have you applied the command to "Go!" in your life? If you have yet to "go," when and how will you follow Jesus' command?

The instruction to baptize and teach was given to all Jesus' followers, not just the apostles and church leaders. Do you feel comfortable both baptizing and teaching others? Why or why not?

Do you believe Jesus' promise to be with us until the end? How does it make you feel?

CHAPTER TEN

Word Eight

"It is not for you to know the times and seasons…
you will receive power when the Holy Spirit has come
upon you, and you will be my witnesses… to the end
of the earth."

Don't miss the little words.

"Then [He appeared] to *all* the apostles [emphasis added]." You will remember that the word *apostle* simply means "sent one," and you may remember that there was more than one occasion upon which our Lord *sent* His disciples out during His ministry. In Luke 9:1-2, Jesus launched his final campaign in Galilee beginning with the twelve disciples He had selected prior to the Sermon on the Mount. "And He called the Twelve together and gave them power and authority over all demons and to cure diseases, and He *sent* them out to proclaim the kingdom of God and to heal." Just one chapter but months later, when Jesus was ready to begin His final trip to Jerusalem,

THE EIGHT *FIRST* WORDS OF CHRIST

"the Lord appointed seventy[-two] others and *sent* them on ahead of Him, two by two, into every town and place where He himself was about to go (Luke 10:1)." In verse 17, "The seventy[-two] returned with joy, saying, 'Lord, even the demons are subject to us in your name!'" You will remember Cleopas was part of this group, and that it did not include the Twelve. Paul tells us in I Corinthians 15:7 that Jesus also appeared to this group of disciples, the eighty-four or eighty-six apostles, and it has been traditionally thought that we do not have any transcript of what was spoken in this meeting. We also have no record from Paul of where it took place. Today we could easily imagine it taking place similar to a Zoom ™ meeting, with each apostle in his place of residence and the Lord appearing and delivering the same message to each one simultaneously. Why not? If He can move in and out of closed rooms and show up all over the countryside in a single day, He can surely be in eighty-four or eighty-six places at once!

I'm not sure all such machinations are necessary, however. A close reading of Dr. Luke's Acts 1 suggests to me that Jesus' appearance in Jerusalem prior to His ascension may have included all His apostles. "In the first book, O Theophilus, I have dealt with all that Jesus began to do and teach, until the day when He was taken up, after He had given commands through the Holy Spirit to *the apostles whom He had chosen.* He presented himself alive to them after His suffering by many proofs, appearing to them during forty days and speaking about the kingdom of God (Acts 1:1-3, emphasis added)." In verse 2, He establishes the "they/them" of the rest of the passage as "His apostles," again His "sent ones." Since what follows is just before His ascension and so obviously after His Great Commission on the Galilean mount some days earlier, in which He "sent" *all* disciples within His hearing to "go," it could be argued that *all* His apostles included every believer at that moment. It takes very little imagination, given Jesus' earlier instructions that they were to stay in Jerusalem until they'd received the power of the Holy Spirit and that He was at the end of forty days since His resurrection, that all of the official apostles and not a few of His other disciples were all gathered to see when He would appear and what would happen next. We humans are like that, always up for the next dog and pony show in town.

Perhaps we should here take a moment to clarify two different uses of the word *apostle*. The first is as I have been using it, anyone who has been sent. Synonyms for the word would include *ambassador*, *messenger*, and *missionary*; and because of Word Seven and the Great Commission, we all fall into this category of "apostle." Each one of us has a mission and purpose to fulfill in God's Kingdom. On the other end of the spectrum is the "office" of apostle. Chief among these are the Twelve Apostles of Jesus Christ: Simon Peter, Andrew, James (Zebedee), John, Philip, Nathanael Bartholomew, Thomas, Matthew (Levi Alphaeus), James (Alphaeus), Thaddeus Judas (James), Simon (the Zealot), and God's replacement for Judas (Iscariot), either Matthias or Paul.

While the Seventy (or Seventy-Two) Apostles were indeed sent out by Jesus in Luke 10 with authority over disease and demons, it is primarily in the tradition of the Eastern Church that these men carried an additional authority in the foundation of the early church in that they were either evangelists, early martyrs, or the "messenger"/ bishop or overseer of the church in various cities and regions around the Mediterranean region of the world. In this tradition, the first missionary to a particular locale is considered to be that area's "apostle" and exercises spiritual authority in that place. It is this notion of "apostolic authority" that attracts those who often turn out to be "false apostles" as Paul mentioned in II Corinthians 11:13 (Demas is mentioned out of the first Seventy in II Timothy 4:10 as one who had been a "fellow worker" with Paul in Philemon 1:24 and Colossians 4:14 but who, out of love for things of the world, deserted Paul in prison and left the faith.) Anyone can *say* he is sent on a mission from Christ, but Jesus reminds us in Matthew 7:16 and 20 that we will recognize the truth of a person's claim by his fruit, the results of his deeds and actions.

Continuing in Acts 1:6-8: "So when they had come together, they asked him, 'Lord, will You at this time restore the kingdom to Israel?' He said to them, 'It is not for you to know times or seasons that the Father has fixed by His own authority, but you will receive power when the Holy Spirit has come upon you, and you will be My witnesses in Jerusalem and in all Judea and Samaria and to the end of the earth.'" My goodness, but it's difficult to let go of a preconceived notion! The Jewish mindset for so long had been that Messiah would come to free Israel from the oppression of other nations; and even after Jesus' death and resurrection, they could not see that Jesus had come to free their oppressors from sin and death as much as He'd come to free them! Still, we who long for Christ's coming soon to rescue us from this fallen world dare not throw stones: I often find myself asking, "How long, O Lord, how long?" while not giving a thought to those who have not yet come to know Jesus as their Lord and Savior. We must walk by faith, trusting the Father that He has fixed times and seasons for all His plans (Ecclesiastes 3:1-8).

As we have already seen in Words Four and Seven, it appears to be imperative that the apostles understand that Jesus *is* going to send the Holy Spirit as He promised. I don't think Jesus thought anyone doubted His promise; I think the fact was just so important to Him that He felt the need to repeat it again and again. Jesus simply knew it's impossible for us to make disciples without the Holy Spirit guiding and directing us. It's certainly impossible to pray and expect healing and even more impossible to cast out demons without the power of the Holy Spirit in our lives. It's impossible to understand or make sense of God's Word unless the Holy Spirit reveals its truth to us. We need the Holy Spirit to convict the world of sin and faithlessness, of righteousness and who Jesus is (since He's no longer with us), and of judgment and who our Accuser is (John 16:8). The Apostle Paul tells us in II Corinthians 1:22 that God seals us with His Holy Spirit and places Him in our hearts as a guarantee that every promise Jesus ever gave us is yes and amen and will come true!

Finally, Jesus gives His apostles a road map, a general set of directions concerning where He is sending them. This time, the epicenter is not the Garden, not the Ark, not the Tower of Babel, and not Ur. This time, the epicenter is Jerusalem, the very center of the Hebrew world and culture. The answer to their deepest longing is not an autonomous state of Israel. The answer to their deepest longing will be as the source of the Universal Creator's desire to have a relationship with each and every person on the planet. They are to begin by sharing this good news with Jews, with their brothers and sisters and neighbors and coworkers and, yes, even their enemies in Jerusalem. From there, they are to go into Judea, to people like them in their love and zeal for God, to people with shared values and histories and interests, to people with whom they can readily identify and who can readily identify with them. From there, they are to reach out to their enemies in Samaria, those people who perhaps once had some similarities to them but have grown away from their roots, people who have intermingled and intermarried with unbelievers or even anti-believers, and people who have taken on a lot of characteristics of the world's culture around them. Samaria will be a true testing ground, not only of their faith, but especially of their love for others, especially for those who are unlovely and antagonistic. Finally, from Samaria, they are to go to the very end of the earth, out into every country, culture, tribe, and nation, wherever the Holy Spirit leads them to go, until the whole world knows of Jesus and His story, of Jesus and His love.

Dr. Luke had already recorded where this final Word was spoken in his Gospel in 24:50. Evidently, the apostles had all gathered in Jerusalem; and when Jesus knew that it was time for Him to ascend to His Father in heaven, He led His entourage of over a hundred, perhaps a hundred twenty people, out as far as Bethany but not beyond the Mount of Olives (Acts 1:12). It was there that He lifted up His hands and blessed them with this final Word. Luke says in verse 51, "While He blessed them, He parted from them and was carried up into heaven" and again over in Acts 1:9, "And when he had said these things, as they were looking on, he was lifted up, and a cloud took him out of their sight."

The story concludes in Acts 1:10-11: "And while they were gazing into heaven as he went, behold, two men stood by them in white robes, and said, 'Men of Galilee, why do you stand looking into heaven? This Jesus, who was taken up from you into heaven, will come in the same way as you saw him go into heaven.'" Jesus ascended into heaven and sat down at the right hand of God His Father, and thus ended the first Words of Christ from out of the tomb.

THE EIGHT *FIRST* WORDS OF CHRIST

For Further Contemplation and Discussion:

Do you consider yourself to be an apostle of Jesus? In what ways has Jesus sent you? How would you rate your apostolic effectiveness on a scale of 1-10 and why?

Would you say you're more focused on the Great Commission and bringing people to Jesus or on watching and getting yourself ready for Jesus return? Why? Explain…

What evidence do you have of the Holy Spirit's presence in your life today? How is He most active in and through you?

What is your epicenter, your Jerusalem; from whence will you go? What is comparable to your Judea? Your Samaria? What end of the earth are you most interested in reaching?

In light of Paul's description of "the Rapture" in I Thessalonians 4:13-18, especially v. 17, what did the angels mean at Jesus' ascension (Acts 1:9-11)?

THE EIGHT *FIRST* WORDS OF CHRIST

MICHAEL A. SALSBURY

CHAPTER ELEVEN

The Eight First Words of Christ: A Review

Word One
"Woman, why are you weeping? ... Whom are you seeking? ... Mary…"

Word Two
"Fear not!"

Word Three
"O foolish men, and slow of heart to believe in all that the prophets have spoken!"

Word Four
"Peace be unto you." I: "Receive Holy Spirit; I am sending the promise of My Father upon you."

Word Five
"Peace be unto you" II: "Blessed are those who have not seen and yet have believed."

THE EIGHT *FIRST* WORDS OF CHRIST

Word Six
"Bring some of the fish…come and have breakfast…
If you love me, feed and tend my lambs, young sheep,
and sheep…Follow Me!"

Word Seven
"Go! Make disciples, baptizing them … and teaching
them…
Lo, I am with you always, even unto the end of the age."

Word Eight
"It is not for you to know the times and seasons…you
will receive power when the Holy Spirit has come upon
you, and you will be my witnesses… to the end of the
earth."

EVEN IN TIMES OF GRIEF AND DESPAIR, I trust you have been challenged to seek Jesus as Mary Magdalene did, and to keep searching desperately until you find Him, until He shows up in your life, perhaps not as a gardener but as a friend or a family member or a next door neighbor or a co-worker or a customer or a concierge or a check-out person or a benefactor or a homeless person or a little boy or teen-age girl or a grocer or… a gardener. Jesus with skin on. You may not recognize Him at all, but when He speaks your name, you'll know it to be Him; and you will worship.

I hope you will learn to live without fear in your life. Paul wrote to Timothy, "God gave us a spirit not of fear but of power and love and self-control (II Timothy 1:7)." It's important to question any time we recognize we are experiencing fear in our lives. I often think of how my stomach churns just a bit when I'm waiting in line (usually a long, hot, and steamy line) to ride some new, latest and greatest roller coaster. Am I afraid? Yes. Will my fear keep me from riding? Hasn't yet. Why? I have faith in the designers, engineers, and builders of the roller coaster, and I believe the testimonials of all the riders who have gone before me and survived! True, we are admonished over and over in Scripture to "fear" God, but that is more like the fear I have for the roller coaster creators: as long as I listen to and obey the instructions, make sure the lap bar and shoulder harnesses are all secure with a snug "click" and I "keep my hands and feet inside the car at all times," I am pretty much guaranteed a wonderful ride!

"The fool says in his heart, 'There is no God' (Psalm 14:1)"; that's what makes him foolish. Jesus called Cleopas and Friend foolish for being slow to believe in the Messianic prophecies of God's Word. As you have studied God's Word over the course of this reading, have you found yourself readily accepting Its truth – not necessarily anything *I've* written (though I hope to have remained true to God's Word) – the truth of the Word as spoken by God; or do you find yourself questioning it, asking "Yeah, but, how can *that* even be possible – flesh and blood and *clothes* actually passing through walls or a locked door – harumph, harumph, harumph?" Again, I find it so much easier to "let God be true though everyone were a liar" (Romans 3:4), to accept that His Word is true and adjust my beliefs to fit rather than to try to make God conform to my way of thinking. I believe it works out better for us that way in the end.

Are you at peace? Is your world one of quiet and rest? Psalm 127:2 says, "He gives those He loves sleep." If you have received Jesus as your Savior and Master, you have

THE EIGHT *FIRST* WORDS OF CHRIST

also received His Holy Spirit as a seal on your life and a guarantee of a hope and a future with Him. That alone should bring peace. If disquiet still rules certain areas of your life, check your relationship with Holy Spirit. Perhaps you're in need of renewal…

Are you at peace? Is your world one of quiet and rest? If not, perhaps your faith is at issue. As Thomas learned, it can be hard to believe without seeing; and so far as any of us know, the Apostles Paul and John are the only folks to whom Jesus has appeared since His ascension. Still, you will do well to believe all that Jesus did for you on His cross, in His burial, and in His resurrection. If you have yet to have believed without having seen the risen Christ, I encourage you to turn away from your sin and turn to Jesus *today* and accept His gift of grace and mercy in your life.

Did you have breakfast this morning? Could you have if you had wanted to? Is God meeting your needs? Is He doing "far more abundantly than all that [you] ask or think, according to the power at work within [you]" (Ephesians 3:20)? If so, and you love God deeply and intimately or even with friendly affection, then look around to see how you can care for other members of the flock. Maybe God is calling you to work in the nursery at church or to provide childcare for a working mom. Maybe he is asking you to teach the eighth grade Sunday School class or get involved with your own kid's sports program or the speech and debate team at the local high school. Maybe He's asking you to attend your church's workdays to keep the property honoring to Him or to volunteer at your local senior center or nursing home. Look for opportunities not only to give to local charities but volunteer for them as well. (Yes, they *all* are *always* looking for volunteers!) All of it is a matter of following the leading of His Holy Spirit. Learn to listen for His still, small voice, those quiet yet insistent nudges to your own spirit, and obey what they tell you to do. Follow Him.

Go. Get out of your comfort zone. Look for opportunities to acquaint yourself with and make friends of people who have yet to believe in Jesus. Bond over a common interest – working out or a sport, a volunteer effort, the community music group, some hobby or class – and actively ask God for an opportunity to share the love of Jesus with people around you, in your Jerusalem, your Judea. If you ask for opportunities to bring people to Jesus, you must "always be prepared to make a defense to anyone who asks you for a reason for the hope that is in you (I Peter 3:15)." A basic skill that every believer must know is how to introduce someone to Christ, but the easiest part is simply beginning with *your* testimony of how *you* came to know Him. Anytime you travel for *whatever* reason, keep a keen outlook available for opportunities to help others: for some reason, these opportunities tend to present themselves when we simply obey the first word: go!

Those of us who have been walking with the Lord for any amount of time have likely had some exposure to teaching about prophecy, the end times, and last days. While there is nothing wrong in knowing what the Bible says on these topics, Jesus warned us about getting so caught up in living for the future that we miss living in the present. Leave the times and seasons in the Father's capable hands: you can't make them hurry up or slow down either way. Our purpose is to remain connected to the Holy Spirit, plugged in to the power source, and "abiding in the Vine" (John 15:4) so we will be able to testify and witness

THE EIGHT *FIRST* WORDS OF CHRIST

to what God has done in our lives all the way to the ends of the earth. Don't just give monetarily to foreign missions but look for an opportunity to go and observe and assist in their work first-hand. It may be yours and only your testimony that is designed to reach someone in a completely different culture than yours, but you'll never know if you don't go.

Thus ends the eight first words of Christ from out of the grave.

May you find Him Whom you seek. May you have done with fear. May you believe in all that the prophets have said about our Messiah. May you know the peace of the Holy Spirit in your life. May you be at peace through faith, believing without seeing. May you continue to follow Jesus. May the Holy Spirit direct you as you go, make disciples, baptizing them in the name of the Triune God and teaching them to obey Jesus' command of love. May you move in the Holy Spirit's power as you bear His witness to the ends of the earth. Hear the seven, no, *eight* first Words of the Lord!

For Further Contemplation and Discussion:

What sticks out to you as the most significant comparison between Jesus' seven last words from the cross and His first eight words out of the grave?

Which of Christ's eight sayings out of the tomb has/have meant the most to you in these two months of study?

THE EIGHT *FIRST* WORDS OF CHRIST

Did you learn any fresh, new-to-you insights about the story of Jesus's forty days on earth from His resurrection to His ascension?

Is there a particular country or culture you feel drawn to where your testimony of coming to know Jesus might be particularly effective? If not, I encourage you to begin getting to know the foreign missionaries whom your church supports and take advantage of one of the many short-term missionary projects available. What will it be?

MICHAEL A. SALSBURY

ACKNOWLEDGMENTS

Solo Deo Gloria!

"And we know that, for those who love God, all things work together for good for those who are called according to His purpose." – Romans 8:28

I AM INDEBTED as ever to my beloved Dearlin', Sandra K. Salsbury. Were it not for her encouragement and her need, I might never have made the leap to staying home and becoming a full-time writer. She has spent forty years allowing and assisting me to pursue my creativity and my calling, and neither this nor any creative effort of mine will ever emerge without her beloved influence. Love you, Babe!

"Two are better than one, because they have a good reward for their toil. For if they fall, one will lift up his fellow. But woe to him who is alone when he falls and has not another to lift him up!" – Ecclesiastes 4:9-10

I have long known that writing is a lonely endeavor, and I'm okay with that – I like to work alone – but I've also learned through my theatre work that creativity is well-served by the company of fellow artists. This day has been decades in the making, to which both my wife and my dear Yokefellow-writers-group friend Mary Mueller will adamantly attest. Mary's lifelong encouragement to plop my seat in the chair and "Write, Mikey, write!" has finally paid off! I'm a great believer in writers groups and am indebted to the Mid Michigan Writers for introducing me to my current group of Diane Hammond, Michelle Morris, Laura Bender, and Lenore Troia, perfect examples of "iron sharpening iron." Add to that mix the powerhouse professional Dario Ciriello who guided me through the maze of self-publishing for the first time, and I'm blessed with an abundance of blessed connections.

> "And [God] made from one man every nation of mankind to live on all the face of the earth, having determined allotted periods and the boundaries of their dwelling place, that they should seek God, and perhaps feel their way toward him and find him." – Acts 17:26-27

This book has been an effort of my feeling my way toward God and finding him after being placed for a time in "boundaries of a dwelling place" I would not have chosen for myself. Having "bloomed where I have been planted," I am grateful for the beautiful garden into which I am transplanted. I am grateful for my brother Kevin, who brought us here, and for the flock of God he pastors at Comins Community Church, who have become our extended family for this season. I am especially grateful for the Berean Sunday School class, who have truly become our brothers and sisters over the past couple of years and who have served as guinea pigs for my teaching over the past year.

> "The grass withers, the flower fades,
> but the word of our God will stand forever." –
> Isaiah 40:8.

They may simply have been tired of staring at an eyesore, but my neighbors expressed their concern for us when they asked if they could mow my lawn for me, and I'm grateful. I really will try to do better, guys! Thanks!

ABOUT THE AUTHOR

MICHAEL A, SALSBURY, MFA is an accomplished actor, performer, director, assistant pastor, minister of music and drama, theatre professor, and writer in numerous genres, and has been in love with both Jesus and story since childhood. His deep love for God's Word is nurtured by a devotional practice begun in early adolescence and continued for the past fifty-two years (and counting!) of His journey with Jesus.

In *The Eight **First** Words of Christ,* he continues his life's mission to "Creatively Communicate Christ, coming to be like Him and calling others to do likewise." He and his beloved wife, Sandy, live in tiny Fairview, Michigan, between the Huron National Forest and the Mackinaw State Forest and look forward to every opportunity to visit daughter and son-in-love Kate and Gabe Clemons and their beautiful grandchildren, Gideon and Willamina, in Virginia Beach.

email *mikesalsburyministries@gmail.com*

THE EIGHT *FIRST* WORDS OF CHRIST

Made in the USA
Monee, IL
04 May 2025